Stories
WITH A MESSAGE
for the
primary school

Helping you deal with difficult issues

RACHEL ADAMS

ACKNOWLEDGEMENTS

I would like to thank my family for their patience and support when I had my writing head on, and the lovely teachers who were kind enough to trial my stories with their classes.

I would also like to thank Megan Crowe and the rest of the team at LDA for all their support in getting this book to print, and Robin Lawrie for his hard work on the illustrations.

Stories with a message for the primary school

ISBN: 978-1-85503-589-8

© Rachel Adams 2015

Illustrations by Robin Lawrie

This edition published 2015

10 9 8 7 6 5 4 3 2 1

Printed in the UK by Page Bros (Norwich) Ltd

Designed and typeset by Andy Wilson for Green Desert Ltd

LDA, 2 Gregory Street, Hyde, Cheshire, SK14 4HR

www.ldalearning.com

The right of Rachel Adams to be identified as the author of this work has been asserted in accordance with Sections 77 and 78 of the Copyright, Designs and Patents Act 1988.

All rights reserved. This book contains materials which may be reproduced by photocopier or other means for use by the purchaser. The permission is granted on the understanding that these copies will be used within the educational establishment of the purchaser. The book and all its contents remain copyright. Copies may be made without reference to the publisher or the licensing scheme for the making of photocopies operated by the Publishers Licensing Society.

CONTENTS

About this book — 1

☐ Friendship, social skills and bullying

My friend only — 2
Kim's twin sister Emma is jealous when Kim makes new friends in her absence.

It's good to share — 6
Paul is taught an important lesson when he leaves one of his friends out.

Be nice or look silly — 9
After bullying Will about his head lice and personal hygiene, Jane is in for a shock.

Too quiet to fit in? — 12
Jade feels powerless against a bully and let down by her shy friends.

True friends — 15
Jenny is made to understand the consequences of picking on Tim about his eczema.

Too fat for friendship? — 20
It is the dreaded Sports Day and Sean finally has the opportunity to tell his teacher how he feels when people talk about his weight.

All control lost — 23
Having chosen not to confide in his teacher about being bullied, Gethin takes matters into his own hands.

△ Health and safety

So ill! — 27
James realises that faking illness and missing school is not such a good idea.

Should have said something — 30
Jake's loyalty to his truanting friend leaves him feeling guilty when his friend is seriously hurt.

Should have looked — 33
Todd learns how dangerous it can be to run into a road without looking.

False alarm?   **36**
Jessica assumes that when the fire alarm goes off it is only another fire drill and goes to get her coat.

Moth to a flame   **39**
Lizzy takes some matches from her parents' drawer and the consequences are life-changing.

✧ *Gender identity and sexuality*

I like looking like a boy   **42**
Amy needs her mum to understand that she is not a 'girly' girl.

That woman looks strange   **45**
A child encounters a man dressed as a woman and forms an opinion based on the reactions of others.

Just a happy family   **47**
Keeley is unsettled by the curiosity of the children at her new school when they discover she has two mums.

⬡ *Violence and anti-social behaviour*

If I'd have fought back...   **51**
Tom is worried that he will be considered weak when he is prevented from retaliating against his bullies.

You damage it, you pay   **54**
Chris has to face the consequences when his identity as the school vandal is discovered.

I'll have that!   **58**
Ben's mum discovers the truth about his stealing habit.

Behaviour beyond understanding   **61**
Dan's friends have had enough of his behaviour and discover they are not the only ones.

The Shadow   **65**
After playing violent computer games with his dad, Rick's role-play in school becomes too aggressive.

☆ Anxiety and self-harm

New school — 69
Holly is dreading her first day at a new school.

It's not so bad — 73
Jane looks back to when her parents first told her they were going to divorce.

She doesn't understand — 76
Adam hurts himself when he loses his temper and his parents realise he needs help.

○ Illness and bereavement

So unprepared — 79
Fay is untidy and unprepared for school when Dad goes into hospital but finds it hard to explain her situation.

I can't explain — 82
As his turn in circle time approaches, Miles wonders how to talk about his nan's death.

Always there — 85
A child looks back to before, during and after their mum's death.

Glad it's not us — 88
Mason struggles to talk to the police after a tragic car accident.

⬠ Child abuse

He shouldn't do that — 92
Jamie discovers that 'stranger danger' is real when a man offers him help after an accident.

Dreading it — 96
Lee comes from a violent background and his problems at home are starting to affect his school life.

Index — 99

ABOUT THIS BOOK

I was working in a primary school when I first realised that a subtle approach can be useful when tackling difficult social and emotional issues with pupils. We've all encountered children who can take offence at the slightest hint of criticism or who find it hard to speak up. I love a good story and, as we all know, so do children. If we can use this enjoyable medium to get a message across to a troubled child (even without them realising this is why they are reading or hearing it) then we can avoid confrontation, embarrassment and other problems that a more direct approach can sometimes create.

Each of the following stories is designed to cover at least one area of concern commonly identified in primary schools in a subtle story format and is reinforced with accompanying discussion questions. These can be used as a starting point for opening further discussion and debate or as a written exercise on an individual, group or whole-class level.

The ultimate aim of this resource is to encourage pupils to consider those around them and the situations in which they might find themselves. The stories encourage a deeper understanding of cause and effect, right and wrong, and reward and consequence. The questions at the end of each story also allow you to gain an interesting insight into the thoughts and emotions of individual pupils.

My friend only

The twins Kim and Emma were always together. They sat together and ate together and very rarely played with other children in the class. They looked so alike that even their mum had trouble telling them apart, so their teacher didn't stand a chance! Sometimes they would even swap seats just to confuse Miss Fitzpatrick. They laughed together at all their private jokes so often that, in time, the other children chose to leave them alone. The twins made it obvious that they didn't need anyone else.

One morning, Emma woke up feeling ill. She was hot to touch and felt shivery. Mum took her temperature with a thermometer and frowned.

"Off to the doctor for you, young lady. We'll drop Kim off at school and go straight to see Dr Morris." Mum went to get breakfast ready and left the girls to get dressed.

Kim felt very alone at school. At morning break, children were playing and chatting happily together all around her, having fun. No-one looked in her direction to see the lonely figure sitting at the side of the playground. She wished Emma was there with her; then she could play with her and they would have fun together like they always did. Kim felt like crying.

After break, the class was surprised to find that a new girl had joined them. Her name was Lisa and her family had just moved to the area. Kim thought she looked nice but seemed shy.

"Kim, would you like to show Lisa around for me and help her to settle in?" Miss Fitzpatrick asked. Kim was pleased.

"Yes, Miss." Kim quickly pointed to the spare seat next to her and smiled at Lisa. Lisa smiled back.

By the end of the day Kim had not only made a new friend, but the rest of the class' curiosity about the new girl had drawn Kim into every conversation. All of the other children had included her and Lisa in their games and Kim had loved it.

Emma was off school for the rest of the week. All Kim talked about was Lisa and her family, her interests, her pets, her likes and dislikes. By the end of the week Emma looked decidedly grumpy, and not just because of the virus she had.

Emma felt better by Monday morning and was looking forward to going back to school. She had been bored at home, especially when she started to feel better. She also wanted to see what Lisa was like as she'd heard so much about her. She didn't have to wait long. Lisa was waiting for Kim by the school gate, along with five other children who Emma wouldn't normally speak to.

"Hi, Kim!" Lisa's face lit up when she saw her friend. She couldn't wait to tell her about her weekend.

"Mum's said I can invite you over for a sleepover. The house is still a mess because most of our stuff is waiting to be unpacked, but if you don't mind sleeping by a stack of boxes, you can come. Ellie and Sophie are coming too. It'll be great!" Lisa led Kim away, chatting excitedly about her plans for the sleepover. Emma was left to tag along, feeling left out.

"Kim, you don't know if Mum will let you go yet," Emma reminded Kim snappily.

"I'll ask tonight," Kim said. "Oh, Lisa, this is my sister Emma," she added.

"I can see that, you're identical! Do you like the same things as Kim?" Lisa asked Emma happily.

"No!" Emma snapped moodily. "I don't think I do!" She pushed past everyone and disappeared inside the school building.

"Sorry Lisa, I'll just go and see if she's okay. She hasn't been well." Kim rushed after Emma. Lisa felt upset.

During the morning's lessons, Emma kept looking across to Lisa and Kim.

My friend only

Lisa was in *her* seat. She made a point of angrily turning to face the other way whenever she knew they could see her watching. Kim felt uncomfortable. Both Lisa and Kim were ready to have words with Emma as soon as the bell rang for lunch, but Emma stood up and left the room before they had the chance. They eventually found her in a corner of the playground, alone and looking miserable. When she saw Kim and Lisa approaching, Emma got up and walked away.

"Lisa, this is hopeless. I'll just have to talk to her later. Let's find the others," Kim said. They went off to find Ruth and Beth and didn't give Emma a backward glance.

The rest of the day passed without incident, although Emma continued to look grumpy until home time. Kim and Lisa stayed well away from her and played with Ruth and Beth instead.

"What's the matter, Emma? Are you feeling unwell again?" Mum was concerned as soon as she saw her. Emma burst into tears and only stopped crying when they got home, where she was finally able to tell her mum what had happened.

When she had finished explaining how Kim and Lisa had left her out and how sad she had felt, Mum sighed.

"Emma, you can't keep Kim to yourself. While you were away, Kim was able to make other friends. If you had let her she could have included you, but from what Miss Fitzpatrick told me on the phone you were grumpy all day and Kim gave up."

Emma hadn't expected that. She hadn't thought that Mum might call the school to see how she was getting on and she certainly hadn't expected her to know how she had behaved. Emma fell silent.

Mum quietly left the room, leaving Emma with her thoughts.

My friend only

What do you think?

1. Explain why you think Emma felt grumpy at home listening to Kim talking about Lisa. Do you think she was right to feel like this?

2. Do you think Emma wanted to like Lisa when she met her for the first time? Explain your answer.

3. How do you think Kim and Lisa could have done more to help Emma feel welcome in their friendship group?

4. Describe how you think Lisa felt about Emma when they first met. Do you think this will affect the way she feels about Emma in the future?

5. Have you ever been left out of something? Describe what happened and how it made you feel.

6. What do you think is meant by the word 'jealousy'?

7. Have you or someone you know ever felt jealous of a friend? Describe why.

8. Do you think Miss Fitzpatrick was right to tell Mum about Emma's behaviour? Explain your answer.

9. Do you think Emma should have had more sympathy from her mum at the end of the story?

10. Describe what you think Emma could do when she returns to school if she wants to join in with Kim's new friends.

© Rachel Adams 2015 *Stories with a message for the primary school* LDA Permission to photocopy

It's good to share

It was a bright, sunny morning and Lucy was looking forward to meeting her friends Emily, Paul, Luke and Mark by the supermarket on the way to school. They always met there on a Friday; it was the only day of the week that none of them got a lift to school. It gave them the chance to go into the shop and buy a big bar of chocolate to share amongst themselves as a special end-of-week treat.

The others were already there when Lucy arrived and Paul was the centre of attention as usual.

"Mum bought them for me, the biggest bag they had. You know that advert for them with the children that get superpowers from eating them? You know, the one that says 'they'll make you a hero' at the end? Well, I've got tons of them at home. I love them. Want one?"

Paul took out a handful of brightly-wrapped sweets from his trouser pocket and offered them to Emily, Luke and Mark. They were quick to take a sweet each and, after hastily unwrapping them, they stuffed the squares of fruit-flavoured chocolate into their mouths as if they hadn't eaten for months. Lucy watched their happy faces as the chocolate melted in their mouths. There was still one left in Paul's hand after everyone else had had one each, including Paul. Expecting to be offered the last sweet, Lucy raised her hand to take it, but Paul snatched it away.

"That's mine, I'm saving it for later!" Paul quickly thrust the sweet back into his pocket. Lucy felt silly and upset. Everyone except Paul looked at each other in disbelief at what they had just seen.

Paul stopped as he saw the unhappy looks on his friends' faces.

"What?" he asked, looking innocent.

"You left Lucy out when you were sharing your sweets!" Mark told Paul crossly.

"But it was my last one!" Now Paul was cross. Lucy started to cry and Emily led her away, giving Paul an angry look over her shoulder as she turned.

"What?" Paul couldn't seem to understand what he had done wrong.

Luke and Mark couldn't believe that their friend could have been so cruel to Lucy yet was unable to see how he had been in the wrong.

"Didn't you see how hurt Lucy was when she was the only one left out?" Luke asked.

"You'd already said that your mum got you the biggest bag there was and that you have loads of sweets at home!" Mark added.

Luke and Mark walked off, leaving Paul to realise what he had done. Paul felt suddenly ashamed of his behaviour. He had been so busy showing off his sweets that he had forgotten to treat his friends equally and hadn't considered their feelings.

"Poor Lucy!" Paul said to no-one in particular as he began to trudge after his friends.

It's good to share

What do you think?

1. Why do you think Paul behaved like this?

2. Have you ever seen this type of behaviour or acted like Paul yourself? Describe your experiences.

3. Describe how you would feel if you were Lucy in this situation.

4. Do you think Lucy and the others will forgive Paul for his behaviour?

5. What advice would you give to Paul on how to make up with Lucy and the rest of his friends?

6. How do you think Paul felt about himself when he realised what his friends thought of his behaviour?

7. Do you think Paul will ever behave like this again? Explain your answer.

8. Do you think it would be easy to stand up for one friend against another? Think about what might stop you from doing so.

Be nice or look silly

"Oh, I'm not sitting by *him* – he's got nits *and* he smells!" Jane announced loudly to the whole class.

"Jane! Come here immediately!" Miss James was quick to stop further comments from escaping Jane's lips and took her outside the classroom to speak to her privately.

Will was left to sit alone. The rest of the class didn't have a problem with him; they seemed to understand that his mum did her best for him and all of his brothers and sisters. They understood that sometimes his clothes weren't as clean as they should be and it may have been a while since it was his turn to have a bath. It was only Jane who was nasty about him, only Jane who made him feel sad. She always drew the class' attention to everything that made him feel different.

When Will had first arrived in his new school with his brothers and sisters, he had felt happy enough. He had been too young to bother about how he looked or to take much notice of Jane's comments. He just knew that she always looked smart and smelt nice. She always had the best of everything and was always quick to tell the class about her family holidays or their new car. Today was different. Will had had enough and Jane's behaviour just made him feel upset. He was glad Miss James was speaking to her.

Jane reappeared a few minutes later looking a little red-faced as she quietly sat down. Her usual group of friends tried to talk to her but she ignored them and sulkily turned her back on them until lunchtime.

As no-one really bothered him, Will was able to find plenty of time to watch Jane during lunchtime. It was funny what he noticed as he watched. He noticed that she was always the centre of attention. She had got over her bad mood enough to speak to her friends again, though thankfully she ignored him. He noticed the way she flicked her long hair about as she talked. He noticed how her voice was always the loudest and she was always boasting about one thing or another. He noticed that she never had anything nice to say about anyone. He also noticed that she always seemed to be scratching her head.

In the afternoon, Jane was having her hair plaited by her friend Amy as Miss James read a story to the class. Jane seemed to be enjoying it.

Suddenly, without warning, Amy jumped up and screamed.

"Jane's got nits!" The whole class jumped with fright then broke out into noisy chatter.

"Settle down class, quiet please," Miss James shouted above the din.

Will noticed how red Jane's face was and how horrified she looked as she realised that she had been about to scratch her head… again.

Miss James put her bookmark back in her book and set it to one side. She decided to address the class.

"A nit is the egg of a head louse. Head lice are a common problem amongst children at school and can soon be cleared up with lotions from the chemist, or even just with conditioner and a fine-toothed comb. Most children get them at some point, so stop fussing."

The class settled down again, but Will noticed that Jane's friends were not sitting as close to her now and Amy was no longer plaiting her hair.

Will wondered if Jane would think twice before making him feel the way she did now. He really hoped so.

What do you think?

1. Why do you think Jane wants to draw attention to Will in the way she does?

2. If you had someone like Will in your class, how would you treat them?

3. Would you prefer to be friends with Will or Jane? Explain your answer.

4. How do you think Jane felt when Amy told the class that she had nits?

5. What do you know about head lice and how to treat them?

6. Miss James explained that head lice are common and easily treated. Do you think the class will be more understanding about Jane's problem now?

7. Do you think this incident will affect Jane's treatment of Will? Explain your answer.

8. What do you think Will could do to help himself fit in better?

9. Do you think Will should say anything to Jane about the way she has treated him? Explain your answer.

10. List some things that you do or someone else does at home that help you to be prepared for school.

Too quiet to fit in?

Jade never seemed to fit in. She didn't like to talk too loud or start a conversation with other children who she didn't know very well. She found it too hard. There were times when she wanted to say something funny or interesting, but something always stopped her. She was always too shy or worried that what she found funny would not make anyone else laugh or that she would end up being laughed at for being boring. Instead, Jade kept herself to herself and usually only spoke when she was spoken to. She had some good friends and she felt that she knew them well enough to be herself with them. When she was with them, she would crack jokes and laugh and give her opinions freely.

Jack was always joking around. He was the classroom clown and Jade was a little scared of him. He was loud and full of himself. Even the teacher seemed a little concerned about his behaviour, but he never did or said anything truly naughty. He just never put his hand up when he wanted to speak, preferring to shout out instead. The rest of the class seemed to like him and they all laughed at his jokes. Jade accepted Jack for who he was and stayed quiet. She tried to concentrate and get on with her work throughout the disruption he sometimes caused in class.

One day it all changed. Jack noticed Jade. She was not laughing at his jokes and was not paying him the attention he felt he deserved. Jade was too quiet.

It was lunchtime before Jack caught up with her as she was talking quietly with her two closest friends, Emma and Darcy. As usual, he had a group of his friends with him, all egging him on and hanging off every word he spoke.

"Oi, you! Janet or whatever your name is!"

Jade looked up, unable to understand why he was talking to her like that. Her eyes met Jack's. He was standing slightly in front of his gang, unsmiling and scary-looking.

"Yes?" She looked uneasily at her friends who had both gone very red in the face and were looking just as uncomfortable as her.

"What's your problem, Janet? Too posh to laugh? You're a snob, you are! You're no better than anyone else in the class. In fact, you're worse because you've hardly got any friends. You're sad, you are!" Jack's sneering face scared Jade. The noises coming from his friends were nasty and Jade just wanted to cry. She found it impossible to find her voice as she looked helplessly to her friends for the support she needed. They didn't help.

"You know what? You're not worth it. You'd better join in next time, or else. C'mon." Jack turned and ushered his gang away like a farmer herding his cattle.

Jade was shaken. Not just by Jack and his outburst, but by the feeling that her friends had been no help to her. She felt lost and more alone than she had ever felt in her life. She got up to leave to find a teacher.

Darcy grabbed her hand.

"I'm sorry, Jade, but he frightens me too."

"And me!" added Emma.

Jade pulled her hand away. At that moment she didn't know what to think or how to feel. She just wanted to run away.

What do you think?

1. Would you prefer to be friends with Jade or Jack? Explain your answer.

2. Do you think the boys in Jack's gang are true friends to him? Explain your answer.

3. Do you think that Jack is really as popular with the class as he thinks he is? Explain your answer.

4. Why do you think Jack acts so tough?

5. What do you think Jade should do after Jack leaves?

6. Do you think Jade's friendship with Emma and Darcy will be affected by what happened with Jack? Explain your answer.

7. Do you think you would be able to support a friend if they were being targeted by someone like Jack? Explain your answer.

8. If someone you knew was as shy as Jade, what could you do to help them feel more comfortable?

9. Describe what problems you think Jack's behaviour causes in school. What do you think the school could do to make Jack improve his behaviour in the future?

10. If Jack does not change his behaviour now, what sort of future do you think he will have?

True friends

Tim always worked hard and was always polite. He was happy in school until Jenny turned up.

She had only been in school for five minutes before she noticed the small, red, itchy patches of flaky eczema on Tim's hands and arms. Of course she had to comment on it. She announced it to anyone who cared to listen.

"Urgh! Tim's arms are blotchy! Tim's got scabs!"

Tim could still feel the heat of embarrassment in his cheeks as he thought about the way all the children in his class had turned to look at him.

Until she showed up, no-one had really noticed. Now they noticed because every time his eczema played up and he had to scratch it, even though he knew he shouldn't, Jenny was there to see it first and then give a running commentary to everyone else.

Mum had noticed a change in Tim over the last three weeks. He used to hate her applying his eczema cream, but now he was asking her to put it on for him. She was pleased because at last his skin seemed to be getting better, though she was suspicious about his sudden change of heart.

It was Monday morning and the sky already promised a glorious day ahead. Tim was glad. He really wanted his last Sports Day of primary school to be a day to remember, and he and the others in Year 6 would be responsible for getting the younger children to their races on time. It was so much easier when the sun was shining.

"Hi, Tim! Are you doing anything in Sports Day today?" his friend Jan asked as she caught up with him at the school gates.

"Yeah, I'm doing the sprint, lap race and relay. What about you?"

"Oh, I'm just in the—" Jan was suddenly interrupted by Jenny as she pushed between them on her way through the gate.

"Yuck! Your legs are even worse than your arms. You look like you've been standing in a nettle patch." With her throwaway remark still hanging in the air, Jenny was gone, leaving Tim and Jan to stare after her.

"I've had enough of that girl," Tim snarled through gritted teeth.

"Ignore her, she's always finding something to tease people about. She had a go at me over my braces yesterday." Jan gave Tim her best toothy smile and her metal braces glinted in the sunlight.

Tim looked closely at Jan. Until today, he hadn't even noticed she was wearing braces. She was just Jan, his friend.

Jan was looking down at Tim's legs, which were in full view as he was in shorts for Sports Day. Suddenly he felt very self-conscious.

"Your legs do look sore, Tim. They're covered in little white lumps." Jan wasn't making fun of him; she was concerned.

"I know. They're really itching and stinging. I walked through the field this morning and the grass was tall. My skin has reacted to it. Mum gave me my tablet this morning for my allergies so I should be okay. My skin is just really sensitive to grass. It'll calm down. Jenny doesn't even try to understand."

Jan placed her hand on Tim's shoulder.

"No, Tim, but your friends do," she said, her eyes full of care.

They were in separate classes in school and split up in the corridor. Jan disappeared into room T3 and Tim trudged into T4 to find Jenny already the centre of attention, telling the assembled crowd of gossiping girls about his legs. His arms were starting to itch now too but he willed himself not to scratch them. He didn't want to give the girls more reason to tease him.

Miss Burton soon arrived to instruct them all on what would happen next. The class settled into an excited hush, all dreaming of winning every race for their team and being crowned 'Athlete of the Year' at next Monday's end-of-term assembly.

Out on the field, Tim had to sit on a chair as usual while the rest of the pupils sat cross-legged on the grass. He knew that it was for the best because if his skin came into contact with grass again it would flare up immediately. The fact that Tim was on a chair seemed hilarious to Jenny, who couldn't resist pointing and whispering to her little gang. Tim tried not to care. He tried not to react as he waited for his name to be called for the sprint. He didn't want to do anything wrong – it would have pleased Jenny too much to see him being told off for saying or doing the wrong thing while he was fighting back.

When his name was called, he ignored her comments and focused on Jan and the rest of his friends who were all looking expectantly at him.

Miss Burton stood by the starting line with the starting pistol. The crowd hushed and Miss Burton spoke loud and clear.

"On your marks, get set..." CRACK! The pistol sounded and Tim was off.

The breeze blew his hair back off his face and cooled his itchy skin. The sense of freedom pushed him on ever faster, ever closer to the finish, until he crossed the line and gradually slowed to a stop amid excited shouts and cheers. He had won. He was sure he had heard Jan's voice cheering him on.

Tim forgot his worries and went on to win the lap race. Then his team won the relay. He felt great.

Over the following week, all talk was of Tim's amazing speed, his talent and his future career as a record-breaking athlete. All of his friends surrounded him and Jenny couldn't get near him to make her spiteful comments.

Monday soon came around again and Tim's Sports Day triumph was yesterday's news. Tim didn't mind. In fact, he had found all the attention a bit embarrassing.

At the end of assembly, the headteacher Mr Hargreaves had an important announcement.

True friends

"I have pleasure in announcing that for the first time ever, we will be having a school prom to say goodbye to our Year 6 pupils before they leave us to go to high school." Tim couldn't hear the rest. The whole hall exploded into excited chatter and cheers until Miss Burton hammered out the first notes of their school song on the piano.

Later, Jan found Tim in the playground, looking very pleased with himself.

"Are you going to the prom?" she asked shyly. Tim guessed why she was asking.

"Not if you don't go with me!" Tim thought he sounded rather smooth and felt even more pleased with himself when Jan's braces gleamed in the sun as she flashed him a huge smile.

"Anyway, I need you to protect me from the dreaded Jenny. She's just been over here asking *me*, of all people, to the prom! Can you believe that?" Tim had been pleased to turn her down.

Tim wasn't stupid; he knew why Jenny had asked. She was used to being the centre of attention and was always showing off. She had only asked him because she wanted to be seen with the Athlete of the Year, the title and award presented to Tim during assembly that morning.

Tim realised that his eczema wasn't that bad after all and felt really good about finally getting even with Jenny.

What do you think?

1. Why do you think Jenny treats Tim so badly about his eczema?

2. What do you think of people who tease others about something they have no control over?

3. Describe what you know about eczema.

4. If someone in your class had eczema, would you be more like Jenny or Jan? Explain your answer.

5. Tim hadn't noticed that his friend Jan wore braces on her teeth because she was 'just Jan'. What do you think this means?

6. Why do you think Tim stopped himself from reacting to Jenny's taunts just before his race started?

7. Do you think that Tim should have forgiven Jenny and accepted her invitation to the prom? Explain your answer.

8. How do you think Jenny felt about Tim by the end of the story?

9. Draw a picture of Jan, Tim and Jenny at the prom. Include speech or thought bubbles.

Too fat for friendship?

Sean hated Sports Day. All his smaller friends loved it. He could hear their excitement through the toilet window. He didn't actually want to go to the toilet, he just wanted to get away from the school field with its brightly-coloured bunting and proud parents cheering their children on in the egg and spoon race.

The toilet was Sean's sanctuary, his escape, his place to think; away from the sympathetic eyes, the rude comments and the feeling that he was different.

Sean hated himself.

Suddenly he heard the outer door to the toilets open with a creak.

"Sean?" It was his class teacher, Miss Rogerson. Why couldn't she just go away?

"Yes, Miss?" Sean answered quietly.

"Are you feeling ill? This has got to be about the fourth time I've seen you come back into school since the competition began. Sean?"

"I've got an upset tummy, Miss," Sean said, hoping he sounded pained enough to get away with his lie.

"Oh, I see. Well, when you can leave the toilet, please come and see me in our classroom. I'd like to talk to you." Sean heard the outer door to the toilets creak open again as Miss Rogerson left. Mr Edwards' muffled announcements over the tannoy muted once more as the door closed.

Sean thought Miss Rogerson sounded cross. What should he do now? He knew he would be in trouble; she must have guessed he had lied to her. Sean continued to sit on the toilet.

At last, he started to calm down. When he had first arrived in the cool shade of the toilet cubicle, his face had been throbbing with the heat of the day and the shame of his humiliation. He had caught sight of his sweaty form as he walked past the mirror. He had been shiny and bright purple and his eyes had looked like two raisins set deep in his bloated face. He had been so drenched with sweat that his white t-shirt was almost see-through. He couldn't seem to stand the heat like his classmates could. He had felt the tops of his legs rubbing together and getting sore. His whole body ached with exhaustion after he had been forced to wobble about during the sack race.

They had thought he couldn't hear them. They had thought he couldn't see the looks on their faces as he struggled. He may be big but he had good hearing and he didn't miss a thing. Sometimes he wished that he didn't hear so it wouldn't hurt him. People forgot he had feelings.

He had recognised the two women. They were related to Myles and Tom, probably grandmothers.

"Oh, poor thing. I'd have never allowed my child to get into that state!"

Sean had heard them clearly from the floor as he had stumbled in front of them for the fifth time. His sack had been too small for him and it was just tripping him up. He had been determined to finish the race though. He made it eventually. Naturally, he had been last, but everyone had cheered loudly as he flopped over the finishing line. He had laughed with his teammates who playfully slapped him on the back as he returned to sit with them. It was what was expected of him.

"Well done, Tubs. Thought you needed oxygen halfway through, though."

"I was about to call an ambulance!"

"I didn't think you could go that purple and still be breathing!"

Sean had laughed and grinned and tried to come up with a witty comeback. It was what was expected after all.

No-one ever saw the pain he suffered at each remark that cut through him and robbed him of his confidence and his ability to fit in. Not one of his classmates was a true friend to him. They were all too busy trying to outdo each other in finding the funniest joke about him. Sean was lonely.

Eventually, Sean joined Miss Rogerson in the classroom. She wasn't cross with him at all. Her eyes were kind and her voice soft.

"Sean," she said, "I know you are very unhappy and I can see how you try to pretend that you're not. I think we need to talk. I want to help you."

Too fat for friendship?

What do you think?

1. Why do you think Sean hates himself?

2. Do you think that anyone should be made to feel bad about themselves by others? Explain your answer.

3. What do you think Sean could do to make himself feel better?

4. Do you think that Sean needs support from anyone? Who?

5. Would you want to be friends with Sean? Explain your answer.

6. If you were one of Sean's classmates, would you find it easier to make jokes about him with everyone else or to stand up for him? Explain your answer.

7. Do you think doing the easy thing is always doing the right thing? Explain your answer.

8. If Sean is always joining in with his classmates joking about his weight, do you think they will understand how he really feels?

9. Miss Rogerson says she knows that Sean is unhappy. What do you think she has noticed to give her this idea?

10. Write a script of the conversation you think Sean and Miss Rogerson should have now. Begin with:

    Miss Rogerson: Sean, I know you are very unhappy and I can see how you try to pretend that you're not. I think we need to talk. I want to help you.

    Sean: …

All control lost

Gethin said goodbye to his mum at the school gates. She kissed him when she thought his friends weren't looking so as not to embarrass him and left him to face what he was sure would be another horrible day. He watched her leave, wishing desperately that she would turn back and take him with her to spend the day doing all the things that she did.

"Oi! Mummy's boy!" Gethin knew straight away that Steven had seen him. He tried to ignore the approaching group of boys and started to walk towards the school entrance.

"Got any lunch today? Mummy will have given you something nice. I'll have it at break. See you by the blue door, loser!" Steven pushed past him, knocking into his shoulder as he led his gang into school.

Rubbing his shoulder, Gethin trudged miserably inside after them to begin another school day.

Miss Peters could tell that something was wrong. Gethin had not been his usual cheerful self for a while. She'd noticed that he was choosing to play quietly on his own instead of joining in with the others. She couldn't allow this to continue.

"Gethin, can I speak to you, please?" she asked as he was about to go outside at break. He was worried about being late to hand over his lunchbox to Steven but did as he was asked. He waited patiently for Miss Peters to begin.

"Is anything the matter?" she asked. Gethin hesitated for a moment. He felt uncomfortable. He was not expecting this.

"No, Miss," he said finally.

"Are you sure about that?" Miss Peters continued.

"Yes, Miss." Gethin could feel his face turning red and he felt hot and bothered.

"Okay. Off you go or you'll miss your break." Gethin turned and left the classroom. Miss Peters watched him go. She was still convinced that there was something wrong but she couldn't help him if he didn't tell her what the problem was.

Out in the cloakroom, Gethin quickly grabbed his lunchbox and ran around to the blue door outside. It was tucked away out of sight from the teachers on playground duty. Steven was waiting for him along with four members of his gang.

"You're late!" he barked. Seeing the lunchbox in Gethin's hand, he added, "Give it to me!"

Steven grabbed it out of Gethin's hand and laughingly proceeded to empty its contents out all over the ground. Steven and his gang jumped on top of the spilt food, trampling over it before laughing and running around to the main playground. Gethin looked down at the soggy mess. His cheese sandwiches and the flapjack that his mum had bought him especially as a treat were squashed flat. His crisp packet had burst and the crumbled remains of his salt and vinegar crisps were stuck on top. His yoghurt was coating everything like icing on a cake.

Gethin felt angrier than he had ever felt in his life. He felt his heart pounding in his chest and his throat felt strangled by a scream of rage that was lodged there, waiting to explode. He ran around to the main playground and without thinking, he flew at Steven. He felt his fists connect with Steven's head, his back, his arms, anywhere he could reach before he felt himself being pulled away.

"I hate you! I hate you!" Gethin screamed hysterically through angry tears at a very shocked Steven. Still struggling to get free, he was dragged into the school building by Mr Thorpe, the teacher on playground duty.

When he had finally calmed down, he was able to talk to Miss Peters about what had happened in the cool shade of her classroom. Miss Peters was shocked to learn that Gethin had been bullied by Steven for over a month.

"I understand how you must have felt. Mr Thorpe has already told me about the mess your lunch was in. I know why you were so angry. Steven and his friends are all in serious trouble and we've already called their parents in about the matter." Miss Peters leaned forward and sighed.

"However, I have to tell you that you're also in serious trouble now. What you did was not the right thing to do either, especially as I saw you moments before and gave you the opportunity to tell me what was wrong. I am very disappointed that you chose not to tell me. Your parents have been called in too."

Gethin sat with his head bowed, ashamed at his lack of self-control. His knuckles were bruised from hitting Steven and he was exhausted. All of his anger and energy had been spent in his moment of rage.

What would his parents say?

All control lost

What do you think?

1. Why do you think Steven treats Gethin in this way?

2. What do you think Gethin should have done when Steven and his gang started to be nasty to him?

3. Miss Peters gave Gethin the chance to explain that something was wrong. What do you think prevented him from telling her what had been happening?

4. Would you tell anyone if you were being bullied at school? Explain your answer.

5. Describe how you would feel and react if someone was nasty to you. Do you think you'd regret acting like this later on?

6. Do you think Miss Peters would have been less disappointed with Gethin's loss of control if he hadn't just ignored the chance to tell her what had been going on?

7. How do you think Gethin's parents will react when they find out what has happened?

8. Explain why you think Gethin was in trouble at the end of the story. Do you think he should have been?

9. Do you think Gethin will be in the same amount of trouble as Steven and his gang? Explain your answer.

10. Consider how Gethin and Steven will feel about each other after this incident. What do you think the school could do to put an end to their problems?

So ill!

James coughed and stopped to listen for Mum. She wasn't coming. He coughed louder.

"Mu-um, I still don't feel well!" he whimpered in as weak a voice as he could manage while still being loud enough for his mum to hear him.

Mum came into his room.

"What's wrong?" She looked suitably worried, much to James' satisfaction.

"I feel really ill again, Mum," James whined pathetically, adding a little cough and splutter for effect.

"I'll get the thermometer to see if you have a temperature," Mum mumbled to herself as she trudged downstairs. She hadn't expected this; he had seemed fine yesterday as soon as it became too late to take him to school. He had begun to feel a little worse last night before bedtime, but she had still hoped he would be well enough for school, especially today.

Mum had an important meeting in work this morning and she really couldn't take a second day off to look after James. She had already been called in to see her boss because of the number of days she had been away from work to look after her son. Now she was worried that she would get into trouble for taking a second day off this week.

Returning to James' bedroom, she quickly took his temperature. It was normal. She took a closer look at him. He was not pale, he was not sweaty or shivery and his cough had suddenly disappeared. She decided to try something.

"I'm just going to call the doctor for some advice, love. I won't be long." She went into her bedroom next door to James' to pick up the phone. James crept out of bed to stand in his doorway so he could hear her conversation better.

"Hello, Dr Morgan? It's Mrs Williams here. I would like some advice about my son. He has been away from school a lot recently for a number of different illnesses and his teacher has told me that he is falling behind in his work. Last

So ill!

month he felt sick and three weeks ago he said he felt like he was going to faint. Two weeks ago he had pains all over and last week he had a bad tummy. This morning he feels ill and has a cough. What do you recommend I do for him? I feel so awful seeing my little boy suffering."

Mum paused. She felt that last sentence was going a little too far, but as there was no-one actually on the other end of the phone, it didn't really matter. She continued her conversation with the 'doctor'.

"So you recommend brussel sprout casserole with braised liver and onions for tea, followed by a large helping of stewed prunes and custard and two large spoonfuls of cod liver oil four times a day? I've just made a note of all that. What about school? Oh, that's good, he'll be so pleased not to miss out as he is very keen to do well. Thank you. I'll tell him straight away."

By the time Mum returned to James' bedroom with a huge brown bottle of cod liver oil, James had washed and changed for school, brushed his teeth, combed his hair and got his bag ready with everything he needed to take with him for the day.

"Oh James, how lovely to see that you're feeling so much better. What on earth could have made you recover so quickly?" Mum asked with relief.

"I heard that the doctor said I would need cod liver oil and thought that perhaps I don't *feel* that bad. I'm just going to see how I get on today," James said as he passed his mum to go downstairs for breakfast. He was starving. Perhaps the maths test wouldn't be too bad after all. Nothing was worth the risk of cod liver oil!

Mum smiled to herself.

After school, Mum noticed how quiet James was as he was eating his dinner. She asked him how his day had been. James paused, obviously upset.

"It was the end-of-term treat yesterday. My class went to the cinema and I missed it!" James started to cry.

"Well, that's what happens when you miss school. You never know what you're missing," Mum said as she walked back into the kitchen to wash up after dinner. She really hoped that James had learned his lesson this time.

What do you think?

1. Do you think that James was ever really ill? Explain your answer.

2. What reasons do you think people might have for lying about feeling ill?

3. What difficulties has James' behaviour caused for himself and his mum?

4. Mum pretended to call the doctor for advice. What else could she have done to help James?

5. Not everyone lies about being ill. What difficulties do you think someone might have on returning to school after a long time away?

6. If your friend was away from school a lot, what do you think you could do to help them feel comfortable in school again?

7. James missed the end-of-term trip to the cinema. How do you think he feels about this?

8. What other things do you think James misses out on at school when he doesn't go in?

9. Do you think that James has learned his lesson by the end of the story?

10. If James had continued to pretend to feel ill, do you think he would have regretted this in the long term? Explain your answer.

Should have said something

Mr Price closed the register and looked around his Year 4 class. They watched as he counted them and then opened the register again. They saw him frown briefly before he stood up to open the door for them to go to morning assembly.

As he was approaching the open door, Jake heard Mr Price ask Mrs Jones, the classroom helper, if she had seen Jonathan. He was ushered out of the door with the others before he could hear her reply.

Jake knew where Jonathan was but he couldn't get him into trouble; it wouldn't be fair. But he could think of nothing else during assembly. When he went back to class, he found he was watching for Jonathan to come in every time the door opened. All morning went by and there was no sign of him, but Jake still kept quiet.

This was not the first time Jonathan had told his mum that he was coming to school only to go somewhere else on his own instead. He said all Jake had to do was keep his mouth shut and no-one need ever know.

After lunch a police officer came into the classroom to see Mr Price, accompanied by the headteacher. The three worried adults left the classroom together to talk in quiet voices out in the corridor. Mrs Jones finished the lesson for Mr Price.

Jake was starting to get an uncomfortable feeling in his tummy now. Jonathan usually turned up at some point, with some excuse about his mum not getting him out of bed on time or having had an appointment. A police officer had never come in before though and it had never felt like Jonathan wouldn't turn up at all. It all felt very strange to Jake.

The bell went for afternoon break and just before Mrs Jones let them out to the cloakroom to get their coats, Mr Price walked into the class with the police officer.

"Children, I would like you all to sit down again, please. Quiet please, settle down. I have something very important to tell you." Mr Price waited for silence. All attention was on him before he spoke again.

"As you may be aware, Jonathan has not been in school today. His mum sent him in as usual this morning and assumed that he was here. We called PC Richards when he didn't arrive. I have to tell you all that a boy in school uniform matching Jonathan's description was seen walking down into the woods behind school this morning. A man walking his dog an hour ago reported seeing a boy lying at the bottom of a steep embankment." He paused. "I am afraid it was Jonathan."

The class gasped.

"He was airlifted to hospital where he is being treated for serious head injuries."

The class gasped again before breaking into conversation about Jonathan. Jake remained quiet. If he had told Mr Price what he knew this morning, Jonathan would have been found earlier. If he had told Mr Price that his friend was taking himself out of school and had been lying to his mum over the past few weeks, perhaps Jonathan would not be in this situation now.

Jake felt terrible. His guilt would stay with him for a very long time.

What do you think?

1. What do you think is meant by the word 'truant'?

2. What reasons could someone have for not wanting to go to school?

3. What do you think could be done to stop children avoiding school?

4. Jake thinks that it wouldn't be 'fair' to tell the teacher about Jonathan in case he gets him into trouble. Do you agree with this? Explain your answer.

5. Jonathan told Jake to 'keep his mouth shut' about him not going to school. Do you think he cared about Jake as a friend?

6. If your friend was truanting like Jonathan, what would you do?

7. Jake feels guilty about what happened to Jonathan. Do you think what happened is his fault?

8. Describe how you think Jonathan's mum and his class are feeling now.

9. How do you think Jonathan will feel if he is able to return to school?

10. What do you think could happen to children who do not try hard in school? Consider what sort of job they could get and how much money they would be able to earn when they leave school.

Should have looked

"Can I go and get an ice cream, Dad?" Todd asked.

Dad was about to pay for their shopping in the supermarket.

"I'm busy at the moment. We'll go and get one after I've put this lot into the car." Dad gestured towards the pile of shopping bags in the trolley.

After the car was loaded, Todd tried again.

"Dad, can I go ahead to the shop and get myself an ice cream now?" He seemed anxious.

"Hang on Todd, we'll go together. Just give me a chance to put the trolley back," Dad replied.

"But Dad, I want to go on my own. It's only over the road and I can see all my friends in the shop already. They're not with *their* dads." Todd was starting to feel cross. Why couldn't Dad see that his friends would think he was a baby for being taken to get an ice cream by his dad? They were all allowed to go on their own; they had their pocket money and their mobile phones and they just went.

Dad could see that this was important to Todd and that he was becoming more conscious of how he looked in front of others. He reached into his pocket for some money.

Anyway, he thought to himself, *I can see the shop from here.*

"I'll just put the trolley away and then I'll go over to wait for you by the wall outside the shop where your friends can't see me, if I'm that much of an embarrassment to you!" Dad joked. "Get me a vanilla ice cream, son." Todd was already making for the edge of the car park. Dad watched as Todd broke into a run as he approached the road beyond.

As Dad turned to park the trolley, he suddenly heard the stomach-churning squeal of brakes. He started to shake as the realisation of what the noise meant hit him. The fear that Todd might have been hit by a car struck him full-force in

Should have looked

his chest. Why had he let Todd run? If he hadn't been running, he would have had more time to judge the speed of approaching traffic.

In a state of panic, Dad ran to the road, afraid of what he would find. As every step took him closer to what he was sure would be a scene of tragedy, his heart thudded harder and harder beneath his ribs.

All of Todd's friends had rushed outside the shop to see what had happened. Dad saw them all, white-faced and shocked, ice creams half-eaten and melting down the sides of their cones.

Dad stopped beside the kerb, alongside the car that had skidded to a halt at an angle in the road. He was too scared to look at the tarmac in front of the car for fear of what he would see. He felt sick.

"Dad!" Todd slipped his hand into Dad's and clung on to it.

Dad looked down in shock to see Todd alive and well, if a little shaken. He didn't care who was watching as he hugged his son to him tighter than ever before.

"I heard the squeal of brakes. I thought you'd been hit by a car," Dad managed to whisper.

"It wasn't me, Dad. Look, it was John. He saw me and ran over the road to meet me. He didn't see the car." Todd started to cry as he pointed to a crowd surrounding a dazed and confused boy propped up against the wall of the newsagent opposite.

Luckily he would survive, but it could have been so different.

Should have looked

What do you think?

1. Why do you think Todd was so desperate to be allowed to get an ice cream on his own?

2. Have you ever felt uncomfortable in front of your friends about having your parents around? Explain your answer.

3. Why do you think Dad was hesitant to allow Todd to get an ice cream on his own?

4. Do you think Dad was right to have trusted Todd to go on his own? Explain your answer.

5. Why do you think John got knocked over by the car?

6. How do you think the driver of the car felt when they hit John?

7. Do you think the driver was partly to blame for the accident? Explain your answer.

8. How do you think John's parents will react when they hear what has happened to their son?

9. How do you think the accident will affect John, Todd and their friends in future?

10. Write down instructions on how to cross a road safely.

False alarm?

"Oh no! Not again!" Miss Okonjo said as the ear-piercing tones of the fire alarm rang out loud and clear for the second day running. Everyone was talking about how the fire alarm should not be going off again. It was only ever tested on a Monday morning and they had had a full fire drill only yesterday.

"Line up quickly and quietly now, children," Miss Okonjo said, standing by the open door to the corridor.

"But Miss, it's raining!" the class whined.

"Leave your belongings. Come on now, quickly, we have to get out to the playground," shouted Miss Okonjo above the din.

The class lined up grumpily, moaning that they'd get wet. Miss Okonjo was having none of it. She led the way to the fire exit where they met up with Mr Stephens' Year 4 class. Jessica noticed unhappily that they were being led away from the cloakroom.

Sneaking away from her class was easy; she was at the back of the line and in the general noise and excitement she didn't think anyone would miss her. Anyway, she didn't want to catch another cold.

It was quiet and empty down the corridor. The retreating sound of excited chatter was becoming a distant hum as she pushed open the heavy door to the junior cloakroom. There was a strange smell in there that Jessica couldn't quite identify as she hurried over to her peg to get her coat on. The smell seemed to be getting stronger and her eyes began to sting. She was suddenly aware of a crackling sound coming from the storeroom at the end of the cloakroom. Her eyes started to water. As she tried to focus on the storeroom door, she became aware of a thin haze of smoke. She was finding it harder to breathe.

Jessica started to cough. The smoke hurt her chest and throat, and her eyes burned as the strong acrid smell reached her nostrils. Smoke began to pour out from under the storeroom door as she stood rooted to the spot, transfixed by the sight before her. She was unable to move and she felt dizzy and sick. The crackling sound was getting louder and she started to sink to the floor, her legs unable to support her any longer.

The door suddenly opened behind her and she felt herself being lifted up and carried outside. She felt a rush of cold air and wet grass as she was placed onto the ground. The fresh, clean air made her cough even more as she tried to breathe it in. She was glad to be out of the building.

Her relief was short-lived. The fireman who had risked his life to hunt for her in school was very cross. He was cross that she had disobeyed her teacher's instruction to leave her belongings. He was cross that she had risked her life to go and fetch her coat, and he was cross that she had caused so much worry to her teacher and her friends. He said that her parents would have to be told. Jessica began to cry.

As Jessica was being given oxygen through a mask over her face, she could hear the fireman telling Miss Okonjo about the fire. He said that it looked as if the fire had started in the storeroom and that the cleaning materials in there had given off poisonous fumes which had poured out into the cloakroom. He said that Jessica had been very lucky to have been found in time, but would have to go to hospital to be checked over.

Jessica started to realise how stupid she had been and how much trouble she was in now.

False alarm?

What do you think?

1. What is a fire drill and why do we have them?

2. Do you think fire drills are important? Explain your answer.

3. Why do you think the children didn't take the fire alarm seriously?

4. Why was Jessica wrong to go and get her coat?

5. What could have happened to Jessica and the fireman if Jessica had not been found as soon as she was?

6. Do you think the fireman was right to be so cross with Jessica? Explain your answer.

7. How do you think Jessica's parents will feel about what has happened?

8. What do you think Jessica will learn from this experience?

9. Write down instructions for what you have to do when your school has a fire drill.

Moth to a flame

Lizzy liked matches. She liked the sound the match made as it scraped against the sandpaper on the side of the box and she liked the instant flame. Her interest had begun on Bonfire Night last year when she had watched Dad light the fuses of the fireworks in their garden. Dad had kept telling her not to get too close to the fireworks so she wouldn't get hurt and had taken the box of matches off her when she had managed to get hold of it. She knew from her dad's reaction that it was naughty to have matches.

Lizzy had always been a daredevil, always the one to disobey her parents, always the one to take risks. When her dad had told her not to climb the big tree in the park, she'd climbed it anyway and had fallen out and broken her leg. Then there had been the time Mum had told her not to eat the last two packs of sweets on the way home but she'd eaten them anyway and then thrown up all over the back seat of Grandad's new car. She had not been the most popular girl that day.

So here she was, clutching the forbidden box of matches. She felt doubly naughty; not only did she have a box of matches, but she had stolen them out of the kitchen drawer when Mum wasn't looking. It had been like an army exercise. She had crept quietly out of the back door, taking care to duck down below the kitchen windowsill, then she'd manoeuvred her way past the shed and down to the bottom of the garden to the safety of her den.

Lizzy loved her den. Dad had made it for her out of leftover wood after he had finished building the shed. He'd nailed the planks of wood to a frame around the base of the apple tree, which now looked like it sprouted out of the top of her den as if by magic.

All Lizzy wanted to do was strike a few matches and watch them burn. Crouching down in the shade of her hiding place, she struck her first match and watched its flame flicker. The ball of yellow light travelled quickly down the wooden matchstick, leaving a blackened trail behind it. It moved ever closer to

Moth to a flame

Lizzy's fingers. She was so busy watching the flame that she didn't notice it getting hotter as it got closer to her skin.

"Ouch!" Lizzy yelled as the pain shot up her fingers. She dropped the match immediately and it landed in the dry grass around the base of the tree. Lizzy was filled with panic. She didn't know what to do. If she screamed, Dad would come running and she would be in trouble for having matches. Standing in her den watching the flames take hold, she couldn't move. They crept closer and closer, devouring everything in their path. Lizzy started to cough. Thick black smoke was billowing all around her as the fire took hold and travelled along the wooden walls of her den…

Where am I? Lizzy thought when she woke up. Her hand and arm were in agonising pain. She became aware of the sound of her mum crying softly somewhere to her left. She carefully opened her eyes and gradually focused on her mum's face.

"Hello, love," Mum sniffed through her tears. "Thank goodness you're okay! You've been very lucky. Dad managed to get you out of the den. There's nothing left of it, or the tree or next door's garden fence. But you're safe now."

Mum's voice was quiet and tired. Her eyes wandered to Lizzy's right hand. It lay like a lump of meat on a mound of special burns dressings, waiting for the nurse to return. Lizzy followed her mum's gaze and gasped. Her swollen arm and hand were red raw and weeping pus from large, watery-looking blisters. It was agony. Lizzy cried, not just because of the pain she was in but also with the realisation that she would be scarred for life. All her dreams of playing the piano and getting her Grade 6 were in tatters. Her fingers were fused together.

Only in that moment did she finally learn that Mum and Dad's warnings about the dangers of matches were not there to annoy her or to simply stop her from doing exciting things for the sake of it. They were there to keep her safe.

Lizzy hadn't listened and now she had paid the price. Now it was too late.

What do you think?

1. Why do you think Lizzy was so interested in matches?

2. Lizzy liked to feel like she was doing something naughty. Have you ever been tempted to do something that you knew was naughty? Describe what happened and how you felt when you were doing it.

3. Lizzy's parents were trying to keep her safe when they told her to keep away from matches. Why do you think Lizzy didn't listen?

4. What do you know about the damage that fire can do to property and the human body?

5. If Lizzy was your friend, what could you have done or said to help her to understand the dangers of fire?

6. How do you think Mum and Dad feel now that Lizzy has been injured?

7. Do you think there was anything else Mum and Dad could have done to prevent this accident from happening?

8. Do you think Lizzy should have called for help when the match fell to the floor? Explain your answer.

9. How do you think Lizzy will feel about matches and fire after this incident?

10. Create a poster warning people of the dangers of fire and giving them advice on fire safety.

I like looking like a boy

"Now look, darling, you *must* wear this dress for the wedding. It's what people expect a young lady to wear," Mum said. She was fast running out of ways to persuade her daughter that she couldn't wear jeans and trainers to her auntie's wedding.

"I am not wearing *that* and I am not a young *lady*!" Amy shouted as she stomped out of her bedroom. Mum looked helplessly at the beautiful dress hanging on the back of the door. It was sky blue. The bodice was fitted to the waist and then merged into a full, floaty skirt of satin with a netting underskirt to fill it out. She had spent fifty pounds on it and a further twenty-five pounds on the sandals to go with it. How could Amy be so ungrateful?

When Mum finally caught up with Amy, she was in her brother's room broodingly reading his music magazines.

Amy looked at her mum angrily then turned away again to read about the first all-girl heavy metal band to hit America.

Mum felt so upset that she couldn't speak. She went away and waited until she felt calmer before talking to Amy.

Amy was in her pyjamas reading in bed when Mum went upstairs for a proper chat with her.

"We need to talk." Mum sat on the edge of the bed and Amy rolled her eyes to the ceiling and tutted. Then she continued to read.

Mum had had enough. She grabbed Amy's book and threw it onto the floor. Amy looked stunned.

"Now listen to me. I will not put up with this attitude any longer. I must know why you don't want to wear that beautiful dress to the wedding. It cost me a lot of money that we can't really afford and—"

"What did you buy it for then? I didn't ask you to!" Amy had recovered the use of her tongue.

"I want you to look smart at your auntie's wedding and I assumed you would also want to look smart with all the family there." Mum found herself shaking with anger but she managed to stay calm.

"You didn't ask me what I wanted to wear though, did you?" Amy said quietly.

"Every time I asked you what type of dress you wanted you wouldn't talk about it. The wedding is tomorrow and if I hadn't got you something you wouldn't be able to go." Mum had been through this so many times she was fed up of saying it.

"Dress! That's it all the time. Dress! I want to wear trousers. When do you ever see me in anything other than trousers? I wear trousers to school, trousers to the park, trousers to go shopping. *I wear trousers!*" Amy had started to raise her voice but was trying to stay calm.

"Look, Mum. I just don't like all the girly stuff. I like hanging around with the boys and playing football with them. I don't fit in with the girls like people think I should and I don't want to look like one. Some girls are okay and some of them are pretty but it doesn't mean I want to be like them, okay? Do you understand?" Amy reached down to pick up her book, all the time searching her mum's face for an indication that she did truly understand.

Mum couldn't speak. She looked as if she'd been smacked in the face with a soggy tea towel, but as far as Amy was concerned, that couldn't be helped.

As Mum left the room, Amy started to read again. She was glad it had come to a head. At last she had been able to tell her mum some of what had been troubling her.

What do you think?

1. Why do you think Amy doesn't want to wear a dress to the wedding?

2. Do you think it matters what Amy wears to the wedding? Describe what you think she should wear and why.

3. Explain what clothes you feel most comfortable in and where you wear them. Do your friends wear similar clothes to you?

4. What is your opinion of girls who like to wear trousers and play games with boys?

5. At the end of the story, Amy is relieved that she has told her mum something that has been on her mind for a while. Why do you think it was important to Amy that she told her?

6. Try to explain how you think Mum feels about what her daughter has told her.

7. Do you think Amy's mum should have reacted differently when Amy told her she didn't want to wear the dress?

8. Write out the conversation that you think Amy and her mum should have had, beginning with:

    Amy: Some girls are okay and some of them are pretty but it doesn't mean I want to be like them, okay? Do you understand?
    Mum: ...

That woman looks strange

The woman in the shop looked different. She wore a nice dress but seemed unable to walk properly in her high heels. Her throat had a big lump at the front and her hair didn't move in the breeze from the open door.

The woman didn't sound like a woman either; her voice was low and quiet when she spoke to the shopkeeper about the weather as he totalled up her shopping on his till. She laughed a strange laugh as she raised a large hand to wave goodbye.

I asked Mum who the woman was and why she looked so different to all the other women in the shop.

Mum told me that sometimes there are men who like to dress up in the sort of clothes that women usually wear. She said that not many men like to do this but some men choose to dress like that every day.

Mum picked some more stuff from the shelves as we carried on shopping. I looked at the other women in the shop. Some were short, some were tall, some were big and some were small. Some women were talking together in small groups. When they said hello to Mum their voices were high-pitched and when they laughed it sounded like a little tune. They were like the women you usually see, even the ones wearing trousers. They put on their makeup nicely and their skin looked soft and their hair looked like it belonged to their heads.

I thought about what Mum had said as we walked to the till to pay for our shopping. I thought about what it might be like to be a man who wants to dress up like a woman. I didn't understand it.

The shopkeeper smiled at me and Mum as he added up the cost of our shopping on his till. He talked about the weather and didn't mention the man dressed like a woman even once.

The shopkeeper knew the man in women's clothing and had not seemed to mind so, I thought, why should we?

What do you think?

1. Have you ever seen someone who you think may have been a man dressed as a woman? Describe what you thought of them.

2. Do you like dressing up? Explain how you think this might be the same as or different to a man wearing women's clothes every day.

3. In the story, the shopkeeper treated the man in women's clothing just like any other customer. Do you think the child telling the story would have thought differently of the man if the shopkeeper had treated him differently?

4. The child telling the story didn't understand why a man would dress like a woman but accepted it anyway. Do you find it easy or difficult to accept the differences of others? Explain your answer.

5. Do you think there is anything about yourself that others may have difficulty accepting? Explain your answer.

6. Have you ever felt different to everyone else? Describe why.

7. What would you say or do if you saw someone being bullied because they were different to everyone else?

8. List the difficulties that you think could be faced by a man who wears women's clothing.

Just a happy family

Time to go home at last. Thank goodness! Keeley had never talked so much in her life. She had spent most of her day answering questions, especially questions about her two mums. The other children had seen them both kissing her goodbye at the school gate that morning. Her new school was much smaller than the city academy she had come from, like Ma had said it would be, but Keeley hadn't realised that everyone would be so nosey.

As the rest of the class were going out to meet their mums and dads, Keeley sat alone in the reading corner. She soon spotted Ma through the classroom window and Miss Davies called to her. Ma came to the door and spoke to Miss Davies about Keeley's first day before they left. Ma held Keeley's hand as they walked across the playground towards home.

"Miss Davies told me you made lots of new friends today. She said you were chatting to everyone. I'm really pleased," Ma said happily as she held open the gate for Keeley to walk through. "Mum will be home soon. Let's go and get fish and chips for tea."

Keeley loved Mum and Ma. To Keeley, her family was like any other happy family. It was all she had ever known. She had always felt very lucky to have two mums. At her old school, her best friend Perry had two dads. Keeley missed Perry most of all. Her school had been one of the largest in the city. It was full of noise and colour and felt like home. Why couldn't Mum have found a new job closer to her old school? That way, they wouldn't have had to move to the country and she wouldn't have had to move schools.

As Ma told her all about how she had decorated her bedroom and described her new curtains, Keeley was very quiet. How could she tell her mums what the others had all been asking about them? How could she tell them how unhappy she had been all day? How could she tell them that, far from making friends, she had just been answering everyone's questions as if she had to defend herself?

Just a happy family

After picking at her fish and chips, Keeley decided to go to bed early. Her mums had a lot to talk about anyway; it had been Mum's first day at work and she had talked about it non-stop since she had arrived home.

Keeley lay still in bed, listening to the ticking of her bedside clock and the faint sound of the television downstairs. At last she had a chance to think about her day properly without her thoughts being interrupted. At last she could try to make sense of how she felt.

Jonathan had seen her last weekend with her mums in the park and he had told everyone that they had been holding hands. Everyone was interested in what he had to say. He was the first to ask questions.

"Who were those ladies I saw you with?" he had asked.

"They're my mums," Keeley replied helpfully.

"Why have you got two mums?" he went on as the other children crowded around.

"They're my family," Keeley answered carefully.

"Which one is your real mum?"

"They're both my real mums, but the one with curly hair gave birth to me."

"Why were they holding hands?"

"They love each other."

"What do you call them both?" Sophie had joined in.

"I call one Mum and the other one Ma," Keeley replied, wondering when the questions would stop.

"Do you live with them both?" Morgan asked.

"Yes." Keeley tried not to sound upset that everyone was listening.

"Have you got a dad?" Ellis asked.

"I've never known my dad."

"Do you like having two mums?" Ramesh asked.

"Yes."

"Don't you want a dad?" Kyle asked.

"I don't know," Keeley had answered uncomfortably.

"Do they sleep together in the same bed?" Jonathan asked.

"Yes." Keeley hoped this would stop soon.

Just a happy family

"Don't you think that's weird?" Finn asked.

"No." Keeley felt a tear roll down her cheek.

It had seemed as if it would never end, and perhaps it wouldn't have if she hadn't started to cry. Keeley still couldn't understand why they had to ask so many questions. In her last school, people weren't so nosey. They understood without having to ask because there were other children who had two mums, or two dads like Perry did.

She was dreading tomorrow.

When Keeley woke up the next day, she felt awful. Her head felt heavy and she had an ache behind her eyes that made it hard to open them. Her stomach felt tight when she thought about having to go to school and she hardly touched her breakfast. Ma looked worried but she said nothing on the walk to school and only waved briefly from the playground as Keeley went inside at the same time as Sophie. They walked together into the cloakroom to take off their coats.

"Keeley, where's your other mum today?" Sophie asked as she hung her coat up on the peg next to Keeley's.

Keeley sighed, wondering if this was the start of another day of questions.

"She went to work early today. She only came yesterday because it was my first day here," Keeley answered, unsure of what Sophie would say next. Would she make fun of her? Would she start asking even more questions?

"That was nice of her. My dad didn't come to see me off when I started," Sophie said before grabbing Keeley's hand and leading her into the classroom to sit in the reading corner with the others. They all chatted to her as if she had always been their friend. No-one mentioned her mums and no-one asked her any more questions. Keeley even managed to laugh out loud with them all when Jonathan fell off his beanbag when he sneezed.

Perhaps they hadn't been nosey after all. Perhaps they had just been curious about something that was new to them.

What do you think?

1. Why do you think the children in Keeley's new school asked so many questions about her mums?

2. Do you think there is a difference between being nosey and being curious? Explain your answer.

3. What questions would you have liked to ask Keeley if you were in her class?

4. How do you think Keeley felt when everyone questioned her about her mums? Explain your answer.

5. Do you think the children in Keeley's class knew how they made Keeley feel with their questions? Explain your answer.

6. Why do you think Keeley didn't tell her mums how she really felt after her first day at her new school?

7. How do you think Keeley's mums would have reacted if they had known what had really happened in school?

8. Describe how you think Keeley felt before and after her second day at school.

9. If you were in Keeley's new class, what could you do to help her feel more comfortable?

10. Describe how you would feel if your friend had two mums or two dads like Keeley and Perry.

If I'd have fought back...

"No Tom, don't! Come with me," Andrew said, struggling with his friend who was fighting to get out of his grasp and into the playground in pursuit of James. Tom was angry and crying in pain. He was shaking like a leaf.

"Come on Tom, he's not worth it!" Andrew forced him to sit back on a cloakroom bench. He was out of breath from the effort of protecting his friend from himself. As he sat down beside Tom, Mrs Smith rushed into the cloakroom with Jake, another boy from their class.

"What happened, boys? Jake said there's been a fight!" Mrs Smith had been running and her face was red. Tom spoke before Andrew could.

"James attacked me!" Tom was still shaking and he was holding his knee. Mrs Smith could see that he was telling the truth.

"Jake saw some of it happen and came to get me. What happened, Tom?"

The boys told Mrs Smith the whole story. Earlier in the day, Tom had accidentally knocked into James in the classroom. He hadn't meant to do it and had apologised straight away. Despite this, James had been nasty to Tom all morning. Finally, at lunchtime, James had followed Tom and Andrew into the cloakroom when they were putting their lunchboxes away. When Andrew had gone to the toilet, James attacked Tom without warning. He had grabbed Tom by his collar and put him in a headlock, demanding an apology. When Tom said that he had already apologised, James kicked his leg hard.

"… and it really hurt!" Tom sobbed to Mrs Smith.

Mrs Smith sent Jake back out of the cloakroom to ask another member of staff to bring James inside while she and Andrew helped a shaken Tom to the staff room.

Tom hobbled all the way there, complaining that he should have fought back and beaten James up and hurt him as much as he had been hurt. Now he was worried that he'd be seen as soft and James would always think of him as an easy

If I'd have fought back...

target. Tom was so upset that he found it difficult to calm himself down and had to sit quietly in the staff room while the headteacher, Mr Stringer, spoke to Jake, Andrew and James.

As Tom and Mrs Smith entered the headteacher's office later, a very tearful James was made to apologise to Tom before being pushed out of the door by his angry parents, who had been called in after lunch. They were telling him off outside in the corridor as Mr Stringer's door closed behind them.

Tom sat down in the big chair in front of the headteacher's desk, feeling small. His leg still hurt and he was glad that Mrs Smith was by his side. Mr Stringer began talking.

"Tom, I have seen Jake and Andrew who have given me their version of events and James has now admitted what he did. He has been suspended from school and I daresay he will also be punished by his parents. I have called your parents too and your mum will be picking you up shortly to take care of you at home."

"I should have fought back!" Tom burst out angrily.

"If you had, it would have made everything a lot worse. Someone could have been seriously injured. You would have ended up in trouble for fighting too. However, by just defending yourself, you have maintained your high standards of behaviour and your dignity. You can't be accused of wrongdoing in any way. I am proud of the way you conducted yourself. Fighting is never the answer."

"But he really hurt me and I let him," Tom said, still distressed.

"Tom, how do you think it would have looked if you had injured James and only you and Andrew had been present? James could have accused you both of ganging up on him. It would have looked like two against one and it would have been difficult to know who to believe. But you were mature enough to deal with the situation as you should have done. You only defended yourself and got help and now James is in trouble, not you!"

Tom thought for a moment and could finally understand what Mr Stringer was trying to say. James had made him angry, and who knows how badly he could have hurt James in his temper?

"Yes, Mr Stringer, I see now," Tom said thoughtfully.

What do you think?

1. What do you think could have made James behave the way he did towards Tom?

2. What could make you feel so angry towards another person that you would want to attack them?

3. What would you do if someone like James attacked you?

4. What do you think would have happened if Andrew had not stopped Tom from going after James?

5. Do you feel the school dealt with the situation fairly? Explain your answer.

6. How do you think the class will feel about James when he returns to school after his suspension?

7. How do you think the class will feel about how Tom, Andrew and Jake dealt with the situation?

8. How do you think James' parents will feel about the way he has behaved?

9. If you were James' parent, what would you do or say to make sure that he understands what he did wrong?

10. After speaking to Mr Stringer, how do you think Tom will behave in similar situations in the future?

You damage it, you pay

Chris was always doing it. Today he'd already scratched his mark on the new dinner table he was sitting at. In fact, Chris' mark of *Chris x LOL* was written on practically every piece of furniture in the school. He'd even carved it on the fence outside and the old oak tree in the park.

He was writing on the wooden shed door at the side of the playground with his permanent marker pen when his friend Tracey came over and nudged his arm by accident. Chris was really angry; the writing now looked more like *Chris x LOV*.

"What did you do that for, stupid?" he shouted at her.

"Stupid? What's more stupid than spoiling everything for everyone else?" Tracey was hurt and walked off in a temper. Chris could be so rude.

Chris watched her go crossly, then looked back at his spoiled masterpiece. He tried to turn it into something artistic instead, but it didn't really work.

The next day, during morning break, Chris was sorting his pencil case out down in the playground. He'd already used up two of his dad's permanent marker pens and threw them in the bin. He liked permanent markers because they never wore off.

"Christopher! I would like to see you in my office!"

Chris jumped. Mrs Parkinson, the headteacher, never left her office to come into the playground. This sounded serious.

When they reached her office, there was a man in overalls leaving just in front of them. He was with Mr Ford, the deputy head. They didn't look at all happy.

Mrs Parkinson did not allow Chris to sit down. Standing awkwardly in front of her desk, Chris listened as she explained that the man with Mr Ford worked for the company they ordered furniture from. He had left a new style of dining table in the school dinner hall last week for the school to sample before deciding whether or not they wanted to order six more.

"Unfortunately, as the table is now damaged, we will have to buy it. I have been told that the writing scratched onto the surface was your doing. Our caretaker also informs me that over the last few weeks you have damaged a number of other items about the school. Your dad is on his way and when he arrives, all of the furniture you have graffitied, the fence, the shed door and the new dinner table will be shown to him. He will need to know what he will be paying for when I give him the bill for the damage you have done. You will have to clean off as much of the mess as possible with a special chemical spray. I hope for your sake it comes off as it will leave less for your dad to pay for."

Chris gulped. He had never expected to be caught. There were nine other boys called Christopher in his school.

"What do you have to say for yourself?" Mrs Parkinson asked.

"Miss, apart from the table, other people had already written all over everything anyway. I was just adding to it. They were spoilt anyway," Chris said defiantly. Mrs Parkinson's face became very red.

"I cannot believe what I'm hearing. What you have done is vandalism. Do you think the school can afford to buy new furniture every time someone comes along with a pen and scribbles on it? It only takes one silly person to damage a clean surface just like you damaged the table and others immediately think 'Oh, that's okay then, I'll just add to it!' That's okay with you, is it? Because it's not okay with me, it's not okay with the school governors and it's not okay with the other children who have to put up with their school being ruined by one silly boy. They don't want to sit at desks that are scribbled on or on seats covered in graffiti." Mrs Parkinson paused, looking angry.

"Someone has also carved a rude message into one of the doors in the boys' toilets. Was that you too?" Mrs Parkinson was leaning so far forward in her chair that Chris was worried she might tip over.

"N—n— no, Miss!" Chris stammered. He was worried now. He had seen the message and it was so rude that it had shocked him.

"But what proof do I have that it wasn't you? If you are capable of the damage you have caused, then you have to see that it is hard for me to believe that you are not guilty of *all* the damage. Now, wait outside my office until your father gets here."

Chris went to stand outside her office, worrying that the whole school would know about what he'd done when they saw him scrubbing his graffiti off the furniture. Then a dreadful thought hit him. Chris gasped.
What will Dad say?

What do you think?

1. Have you or someone you know ever damaged the property of others? Describe what happened.

2. Why do you think people graffiti?

3. Would you rather sit at a clean desk or one that has graffiti on it? Explain your answer.

4. Do you agree with Chris that it is okay to write on surfaces if they already have graffiti on them? Explain your answer.

5. Chris didn't think that he would get caught because there are other people called Christopher in his school. What do you think he would have done if someone else was made to take the blame?

6. How do you think Mrs Parkinson knew that Christopher was responsible for the graffiti?

7. Why do you think Mrs Parkinson was so angry with Chris' answer when she asked him if he had anything to say for himself?

8. If you had a friend who was behaving like Chris, would you tell a teacher or not? Explain your answer.

9. How do you think Chris' dad should punish him for his behaviour?

10. Write a letter of apology from Chris to his headteacher.

I'll have that!

The shiny red metal car glistened as it sped across the building block bridge and glided down the book ramp, through the cardboard tunnel and out across the carpet.

Ben had taken ages to make the circuit for the car to travel along and it was the best he'd ever made. It went under the sofa, across the rug in front of the fireplace and under the coffee table. It was terrific! He was so busy playing that he hadn't noticed his mum watching him quietly from the doorway.

"Ben, that's a nice car. I don't remember that one," Mum said. Ben nearly jumped out of his skin and looked up sharply to lock eyes with his mum.

"Oh, hi Mum. It is nice. It's an old one I'd forgotten about." Ben struggled to get his words out. Mum noticed.

"It looks just like the one that Gary had yesterday in school. The one he lost. The one his dad gave him for his birthday," Mum said suspiciously.

"Oh. I can't remember that one!" Ben tried to sound innocent and was relieved when his mum left him alone to play again.

Mum was worried about the sudden appearance of the car and decided to go upstairs to Ben's room and check his school bag to set her mind at ease. She hated the thought that Ben might have taken the car from his friend at school, but what other explanation could there be? She was certain the car was not one that she or anyone else had given him. She had to check.

Picking her way through the soft toys and discarded clothes covering Ben's bedroom floor, she eventually uncovered his school bag. It had been flung in the corner next to his wardrobe when he had come home yesterday and had been buried beneath his pyjamas.

The bag felt heavy, even though it should have been empty. His reading book was downstairs and Ben had given her his lunch box and drink bottle out of it before he had gone upstairs yesterday. Mum wondered what on earth could be in it. On opening the front compartment, she was relieved to see a collection of odd-shaped stones. She knew that Ben loved to collect little treasures like these. Mum took a deep breath as she opened the large compartment. Inside was the shiny blue gift bag that Gary had taken his car to school in.

Mum was horrified. To make it worse, there was also a watch, a book from the school library stamped 'Do Not Remove' in bold black print, a can of fizzy drink which she never allowed Ben to have, and a pack of biscuits that were not a brand she normally bought.

Mum sat down on Ben's bed. She was shaking and she felt sick. Not only had Ben lied to her, but he had also stolen from his friend, from school and, for all she knew, from the local shop as well.

Sitting alone in Ben's bedroom, full of everything he could ever want, she wanted to cry. Why would Ben feel the need to take what wasn't his when he had so much already?

I'll have that!

What do you think?

1. Has anything ever been stolen from you? Describe how it felt or how you think it would feel.

2. What is your opinion of Ben after reading the story?

3. When a person steals something, do you think they think about the person they are stealing from? Explain your answer.

4. Why does Mum suspect Ben of stealing from the local shop as well as his friends?

5. What do you think Mum should do after finding out that Ben has been stealing?

6. How do you think Ben should be punished by his mum and school?

7. Do you think that Ben will ever stop stealing if he is not punished for it now? Explain your answer.

8. How do you think Gary and the rest of the class will feel about Ben when they find out that he stole Gary's birthday present?

9. Do you think Gary will ever forgive Ben? List some ways in which Ben could try to make it up to him.

10. Do you think stealing is okay in any circumstances? Explain your answer.

Behaviour beyond understanding

Dan always wanted his own way and he usually got it. His friends weren't really scared of him, but most of the time they just found it easier to keep him happy.

If Dan decided he wanted to use Tom's football, Dan got it. If Dan wanted Graham's last sandwich, Dan got it. If Dan didn't get what he wanted, the other boys knew only too well what would happen.

Only last week he had been refused third helpings of jam tart and custard by one of the lunch ladies. Dan had thrown his spoon and tray across the nearest table without a thought for anyone sitting there and sworn loudly, using words that his friends had never heard before. He then sat with his arms folded, his scowling face displaying a deep frown, breathing heavily. The lunch supervisors had tried to coax him outside so they could clear away, but he refused to move. It took over an hour and the headteacher using his best angry voice before they could finally get him into a classroom.

Now, at the start of a new week, Dan had not arrived in a good mood. His friends were used to it; it was nothing new. It was morning break before Dan spoke to anyone and when he did, it was to demand that Jack give him one of his snack bars. Jack did as he was told, but only because he knew it was easier than making Dan angry. When Dan went to sit on his own at the end of the playground, Jack went to find the rest of his friends around the corner by the caretaker's shed.

"I've just had to give Dan one of my snack bars. I was going to save it to have after school before going to football." Jack felt really cross with himself for just giving in. Dan always made him feel that he had to. The other boys sighed and seemed to feel the same as Jack.

"I've had enough. I'm not giving in to him anymore," Jack said suddenly, sounding brave until he thought about what he had just said. Then he quickly added, "What do you think he'll do?"

The others just looked at him. There was really no need for them to answer. They all knew what Dan would do – he would fly into the most horrible rage and would end up swearing and shouting and lashing out at whoever was nearby. Dan used words that none of the other boys would ever dream of using.

Just then, Jack and the rest of the group heard a commotion and ran to the playground to see what it was all about. Dan was refusing to pick up the snack bar wrapper that he had dropped by the side of the playground. He was shouting at the top of his voice at Miss Diaz because she had tried to get him to put it in the bin. Dan was now so angry that his face was very red. Jack watched as Dan ran away from Miss Diaz across the playground and tried to climb over the school wall in an attempt to escape. Miss Diaz sent Harry inside to fetch Mr Peel.

The whistle blew and everyone fell silent. Mr Peel was already aware of Dan's behaviour and made his way across the playground in a few quick strides. He told everyone to make their way back into school, class by class.

Back inside, they all started to grumble that it was unfair that they had to miss the last ten minutes of playtime thanks to Dan. Mr Peel had to stay outside in the playground with Dan so his class had to be taken by Mrs Walker in his absence.

Mr Peel joined the class just before lunchtime, closely followed by Dan. No-one spoke to Dan but all eyes followed him to his seat, where he sat not speaking to anyone and not looking up from the desk in front of him. Before long, a lady turned up to pick him up from school and Dan got up from his seat to go, determined not to look at any of his classmates. He left the room, closing the door quietly behind him.

Mr Peel asked the class to clear away early for lunch as there was something he needed to say. Curiosity spurred the children on to clear up in double quick time and wait expectantly for Mr Peel to speak.

Nothing could have prepared them for what came next.

"I could not let this morning's incident pass without comment," Mr Peel began. "Dan has behaved badly at times since he joined us, but I would like to thank you for trying to be good friends to him. Unfortunately, Dan is now leaving our school. He was only ever going to be with us for a short time anyway.

"I don't expect to see any of you behaving badly towards staff or each other and I don't expect to hear you swearing. Just because you know these words now does not mean that you have to use them. I like to think you are all much better than that!" Mr Peel paused and breathed in deeply.

"Now, I think you deserve a little extra playtime to make up for your morning break being cut short. Out you go." Mr Peel rose with the class to walk with them down to the playground.

The class were excited to have this unexpected extra break and practically skipped out of the classroom to the fresh air outside.

Jack and his friends walked slowly at the back of the excited, chattering group of children. They were all thinking about Dan and all the things that Mr Peel hadn't said.

What do you think?

1. Why do you think Dan behaves like he does?

2. Do you think there are always reasons for bad behaviour? What could they be?

3. Do you think that Dan has any control over his behaviour? Explain your answer.

4. What do you think could make Dan want to behave better?

5. Do you know anyone who uses swear words? Describe what you think of them.

6. What do you think of Dan's friends after reading the story? Explain your answer.

7. Why do you think Jack and the other boys were friends with Dan?

8. Do you think the school or Dan's friends could have done anything to encourage Dan to behave better?

9. Do you think Mr Peel was right to talk to the class after Dan had left? Explain your answer.

10. What do you think will happen to Dan now he is no longer a pupil at the school?

The Shadow

Rick Miller was angry, his face a mask of fury. His lips were pulled back revealing snarling teeth as he spat out a string of swear words so foul that Alice felt scared and ran to tell Mrs Robinson in the staff room.

Rick didn't care. He was having too much fun terrorising everyone he met in the playground. He was The Shadow, the meanest criminal in the world of gaming. The Shadow was his favourite character from the Vicious Streets series, the video games that only people over eighteen were allowed to play. Rick's dad let him play with him anyway. Rick loved it. He felt really grown up sitting next to his dad, shooting at the screen with his controller. His dad got really excited too, shooting at everything that moved. Rick had soon learned that if he pressed two buttons at the same time he could kill all the good guys in just two moves. It was awesome!

His character, The Shadow, always used lots of swear words, the ones that Dad sometimes used at home. Dad and Rick had played the games together every night since the first one had come out last year. They were the best on the market, according to Dad.

"Ouch! I'm telling on you!" Adam shouted as Rick smacked him on the arm. Adam ran towards school – he wasn't hanging around to be hit again for no reason.

"No, you're not!" Rick chased Adam towards the entrance. He was The Shadow and nothing escaped him. He rugby-tackled Adam just as he got to the path leading up to the steps. Adam fell forward with Rick wrapped around his knees.

"You're dead!" Rick screamed triumphantly as he let go of Adam's knees and started punching his back.

Adam didn't move.

"Rick Miller! Stop that immediately!" Mrs Robinson screamed loudly at Rick as she ran towards the scene with Alice by her side. Rick did not stop. In his head he was The Shadow, and he had to be sure that Adam the cop was dead. Miss Khan, the lunchtime supervisor, arrived and grabbed Rick to stop him punching Adam again.

"I'm sorry, Mrs Robinson, I was on the other side of the playground. I couldn't get here fast enough," Miss Khan puffed, out of breath and struggling to hold on to Rick as she dragged him off Adam.

Adam still did not move.

"Look what you've done!" Mrs Robinson yelled. She was horrified to see a small pool of blood on the tarmac beneath Adam's head. It was gradually spreading. Alice was crying and shaking. Almost without realising it, her small hand had reached for Mrs Robinson's skirt and was clinging to it for comfort. By now Miss Khan was holding Rick tight, pinning his arms to his sides so that he couldn't move. Rick hated it.

"Get off me! I hate you! You're dead! I'll get you for this!" Rick was snarling. Foamy spit was coming from his mouth and he was struggling for all he was worth. "You'll be sorry! You won't get away with this!"

Mrs Robinson could still hear his angry shouts and abuse as she ran to call for help. By now, a small audience of curious children had started to gather to see what all the fuss was about. Mrs Robinson needed two other members of staff to get the situation under control while she rang for an ambulance for Adam.

Adam still wasn't moving.

Later, after Adam and his mum had been rushed to hospital in the back of the ambulance, Mrs Robinson showed Rick, his parents and Miss Khan into her office. She waited until everyone was seated and the school secretary came in to take notes.

Mrs Robinson recounted the events of lunchtime to Rick's mum and dad. They listened quietly until Mrs Robinson had finished.

"I had to send Alice home as she was so upset by what she saw and heard. Miss Khan was punched and eventually bitten by your son in his attempts to get her to let him go. Had she let him go, I firmly believe that Rick would have continued his attack on Adam, who only became conscious again as he was put into the ambulance. He had been knocked out for a full fifteen minutes. The level of aggression that I witnessed from your son was staggering and I am left with no alternative other than to suspend him immediately. I have to seek approval from the board of governors, but I will recommend that Rick is expelled. As you know, this is not the first time we have seen this type of behaviour from your son." Mrs Robinson turned to Rick. "Do you have anything to say for yourself?"

"I was only playing. It was a game. I don't know what the big deal is. I was The Shadow," Rick answered defiantly.

Mrs Robinson looked confused.

Mrs Miller explained quietly about the Vicious Streets games. Apart from an occasional glance towards her husband, she kept her head down. She was very pale and was shaking as she spoke. She told Mrs Robinson about the hour every night that her husband and son spent playing the games.

When she had finished, Mrs Robinson was stunned.

"I have heard of these games and I have to say that any game designed for adult use is not appropriate for children, especially a nine-year-old. Do *you* think they're appropriate?"

"They're only games. It's a harmless bit of fun!" Mr Miller chipped in quickly.

"Harmless? Are they?" Mrs Robinson said, her voice quiet with anger. "*Really?*"

What do you think?

1. Do you play video games at home? Which ones? Describe them.

2. How do you know how old you have to be to play a certain video game?

3. Do you think it is okay for children to play games meant for adults? Explain your answer.

4. Why do you think Rick pretends to be The Shadow at school?

5. Do you think Rick would be different if he didn't play video games at home? Explain your answer.

6. What else do you think Rick could be doing in his spare time?

7. What can happen to people who do not exercise enough or get enough fresh air?

8. Do you think anyone is to blame for Rick's behaviour apart from himself?

9. Do you think this incident will affect the attitudes of Rick's parents towards video games?

10. How do you think Rick should be punished by the school and his parents?

New school

The headteacher seemed nice as he chatted with Mum and Dad. His office was cosy with pictures of his family on the wall. Holly's part in the conversation had finished and now she was left to sit quietly listening to the grown-ups. The sound of singing occasionally reached her ears as the juniors practised in the hall and the smell of minced beef and onions wafted through from the school kitchen.

"So we'll look forward to seeing Holly tomorrow," Mr Harris said as he shook hands with Mum and Dad when they all stood up. Holly smiled shyly at Mr Harris as she stood up by her mum's side. She was desperately trying to look as if she really wanted to be there.

"See you tomorrow, Holly." Mr Harris showed them all out and Mum and Dad chatted happily all the way back to the car. Holly sat quietly in the back during the drive to their new house. Mum asked her a couple of times if she was okay and Holly just smiled and nodded, longing for the chance to sit quietly and think.

As soon as Dad opened the front door, Holly hurried inside and ran upstairs to her new room. It all felt like it was happening too quickly. Dad losing his job back home was bad enough, but having to move miles away from her friends was something she'd never dreamed she'd have to do. Packing up all her stuff into plain brown boxes with little sticky labels on to tell the removal men where to put them in the new house was heart-breaking. And now she was starting a new school, not next week or after half-term but tomorrow! Holly was terrified. Her tummy felt like it wanted to escape up through her throat and her breathing felt fast and shallow. Tears started to pour down her cheeks and drip off her chin.

She really missed her friends back home and wondered what they would be doing. Who would she talk to tomorrow? What if no-one liked her? What if she got lost? What if she got told off and everyone laughed at her? What if she felt ill but they refused to send for Mum? What if Mum hadn't bought her the right

New school

uniform? What if she didn't have everything she needed for the day? Her worries were endless.

Later, after only picking at her dinner, she took herself back to her new bedroom. It was cluttered up with plain brown boxes. She didn't want to touch them, as if ignoring them and leaving them in the heap where they had been dumped yesterday would mean that she wouldn't have to stay here. This house wasn't home.

Holly had a sleepless night. She couldn't get comfortable. Her heart thumped a rhythm of its own in her chest and her head ached with the pressure of all her worries.

Holly couldn't eat breakfast the following morning. Mum and Dad tried to reassure her.

"Mr Harris was lovely. It's a really nice school too," Dad said, almost begging her to be happy about it.

"By lunchtime, you won't know what all the fuss was about," Mum chipped in.

It's all right for them, Holly thought to herself. Their new jobs didn't start for two weeks so they could spend time getting used to the idea, not like her!

Within an hour, Holly found herself standing in a strange classroom in front of a sea of unfamiliar faces, all looking at her.

"Holly will need a bit of help settling in and finding her way around. I know I can rely on you to make her feel at home. Thank you," Mr Harris said with a brief nod and a smile to her new class teacher, Miss Green. Then he was gone.

"Annabelle, Holly will be sitting next to you for the time being. Would you

New school

like to take her out during assembly to show her where everything is?" Miss Green asked with a warm smile.

"Yes, Miss," Annabelle answered politely. She waited with Holly while the rest of the class filed out to go to assembly in the hall. Despite her nervousness, Holly noticed that a few of the children smiled at her on their way out and she was able to smile back. She felt a little better.

Annabelle chatted to her as she showed her around the school. She told her where to hang up her coat, where the toilets were and where to find her work tray. She told her all about what she and her friends liked to do at playtime and what was on offer in the tuck shop. She even offered to lend her twenty pence for an apple if she didn't have any money with her.

By the end of the day, Holly was exhausted. The other children were curious about her. They asked her where she was from, why she'd moved and where she was living. They talked to her and made her feel like one of them. She was made to feel like she belonged.

By the time Mum picked her up, she'd made so many new friends she'd forgotten the names of half of them. She chatted happily to Mum all the way back to the house.

"Mum, it was great! I had a really good day," she said, practically bouncing about in the back of the car.

"Perhaps when you've settled into your new bedroom you can invite some of your new friends over," Mum suggested as she stopped the car outside their house.

"Maybe!" Holly replied happily.

Perhaps this could be home after all, she thought to herself as she hurried upstairs to unpack the boxes in her bedroom.

New school

What do you think?

1. Why do you think Holly was scared of going to her new school?

2. Describe how you felt when you started going to your school.

3. Describe what makes you feel worried.

4. Holly remained quiet about all her worries and didn't tell her parents. Do you think this was the best thing to do?

5. If someone new joined your school, what do you think you and your friends could do to help them settle in?

6. Why do you think Mum and Dad wanted Holly to start at her new school so quickly?

7. What do you think Mum and Dad could have done to help Holly feel less anxious?

8. Mum and Dad also have to settle into the new area and their new jobs. How do you think they are feeling?

9. Imagine you are Holly and you want to tell your parents about all the things that are worrying you. What would you say?

10. List some things that might make you feel better when you are anxious or worried.

It's not so bad

Home had felt different for a while. Jane wasn't sure what the problem was exactly, it just seemed different. Mum and Dad seemed okay most of the time so Jane wasn't too worried, but sometimes Mum's voice sounded a little too bright and sometimes, if Jane walked into a room that her parents were already in, they would suddenly stop talking and one of them would start saying something silly or walk out of the room.

It had been a day like any other day. Jane had gone to school as usual, gone home as usual, helped mum with tea as usual and gone to bed as usual. But the sounds coming from downstairs that night were not usual. The sounds of the telly and the low hum of her parents' conversation had been replaced by Mum shouting in a high-pitched voice. Jane could hear occasional words crisp and clear, things like 'you're not being fair', 'I hate this' and 'don't start'. Dad's voice had been lower and quieter than Mum's and was too muffled for Jane to make out. Jane had been scared. Her tummy felt uncomfortable and she couldn't get to sleep for ages. When she did finally fall asleep, she was tormented by bad dreams.

The next morning, Jane had woken up exhausted with an aching head and heavy eyes. The first thing she had thought of was her parents' argument the previous night. She had dressed hurriedly and run downstairs to find Mum and Dad sat at the kitchen table. They usually had a cooked breakfast on a Saturday, but that Saturday was different.

Mum looked as if she had been crying and Dad looked tired. There were brown circles under his eyes that made them appear to sink into the back of his head. Jane's younger brother Ben was blissfully unaware of everything as he slept dreamlessly in his cot upstairs. Mum hadn't even woken him yet for his bath.

Looking back, it was so obvious that something was very wrong and had been for a long time.

Jane remembered how frightened she had been at the thought of her parents'

It's not so bad

divorce. She hadn't even known what the word meant. Mum had explained that she and Dad could not stay married anymore because they didn't love each other enough, and that a divorce was a way of stopping being married to each other. Mum reassured her that they both still loved her and Ben very, very much though. Jane had cried at first and felt she couldn't turn to anyone. Her little brother was too young for her to confide in and her mum and dad seemed so wrapped up in what they were going through that she no longer felt like she could talk to them either.

That was two years ago.

Now she realised how much better things were. Her parents were happier and relaxed in their new lives. She and Ben had two bedrooms each, one at Mum's and one at Dad's.

It had been strange when Mum had introduced her and Ben to her new friend, John. It had seemed to Jane that John wanted to take over Dad's place in the house, something that she hadn't liked the idea of at first. John had turned out to be really nice though. Not long afterwards, Dad had introduced them both to his friend Lisa and her two children. It had all happened gradually and, looking back, it had not been scary at all.

Jane now realised just how lucky she was to have so many people in her life who loved her and Ben. They even had two older step-sisters who adored them.

The divorce had not been a bad thing at all, despite how it had frightened her at first. At the time, Jane would never have thought that it could actually lead to a lot of good things.

What do you think?

1. What do you think is meant by the word 'divorce'?

2. What reasons might make two married people want to divorce?

3. How do you think parents who divorce feel about their children? Explain your answer.

4. What do you think parents who are thinking of getting a divorce can do to help their children understand what is happening?

5. At the start of the story, Jane thought that things at home 'felt different'. What do you think was happening to make Jane feel like this?

6. If you were in Jane's position, would you tell anyone about the difficulties you were experiencing at home? Who?

7. What do you think Jane would have liked her school and friends to do to help her when she first found out about her parents' divorce?

8. Do you think that arguments between people in a relationship are always bad? Explain your answer.

9. List the good and bad things that have come out of Jane's parents' divorce.

10. Write two diary entries as if you are Jane, one from the start of her parents' troubles and another from now, two years after they divorced.

She doesn't understand

"No, I'm sorry Adam, you can't. There's school tomorrow and it's on late," Mum told him firmly as she cleaned the kitchen surfaces and started to dry the dishes. He could tell there was no way she was going to change her mind. It made him angry.

Adam ran from his mum. He couldn't make her understand; she never understood. Watching Football Fantasy Quiz Night with Dad tonight was essential. All of his friends would be talking about it in school tomorrow. If he didn't watch it he'd be the only one left out of all their excited conversations. Why couldn't she ever understand?

To Adam, it seemed that all Mum ever cared about was getting him off to bed so he 'wouldn't be tired in the morning'. She never listened. Even at dinner, when he was desperate to tell her and Dad about his day, she was too busy telling him to 'eat up before it gets cold' to listen to him.

By the time Adam reached his bedroom, his temper was reaching the point of explosion. He felt powerless and angry. It felt as if his anger was forcing itself out of his throat and his head was full of pressure, making it throb. So Adam did what he always did when he was in a temper, almost without thinking because it had become such a familiar habit.

Downstairs, Mum could hear the familiar *thump, thump, thump* and knew what Adam was doing. With a glance at Dad she grabbed the tea towel from the drainer, raced up the stairs two at a time and ran into Adam's bedroom. She took in the sight before her. Adam was lying on his back on the floor continually hitting his head back on the hard wooden floorboards. He was crying and had started to scream. Mum quickly threw the tea towel under his head to stop him seriously hurting himself and waited for him to calm down.

Slowly, the noise calmed to a sob and Adam eventually sat up. Mum couldn't go near him. It broke her heart to leave his room knowing that he was troubled, knowing that if she approached him too soon she risked setting off his temper again. She chose instead to return to the kitchen and continue drying the dishes from dinner.

"This can't go on, love. I think he needs help," Dad said, appearing from the kitchen doorway.

"I know. I just don't understand why he wants to hurt himself whenever he feels angry. He's even doing it when he simply feels worried. He's got scars on his arms and his teacher even asked me the other day what had happened. I can't do this anymore." It was too much for Mum. She burst into tears.

Mum and Dad comforted each other in the silent kitchen while Adam stayed in a temper upstairs, too angry to care about what he was doing to those who loved him.

What do you think?

1. Do you think Adam's temper in the story is justified? Describe how you think Adam could have dealt with his disappointment differently.

2. Describe the worst thing you have ever done when you have been in a temper and how you felt afterwards.

3. How do you think Adam's temper is affecting his family?

4. Why do you think that some people choose to hurt themselves on purpose?

5. Do you think that hurting yourself on purpose really helps? Explain your answer.

6. Dad thinks that Adam needs help. What sort of help do you think he needs?

7. How do you think Adam will feel about the suggestion that he needs help?

8. Do you think Mum and Dad should inform Adam's school of his behaviour at home? Explain your answer.

9. How do you think Adam will feel about himself when he has calmed down?

10. Describe what you think might happen to Adam if he does not learn to control his temper.

So unprepared

"This is the fourth time you've come to my lesson without your kit! I've got a good mind to send you to lost property to find shorts and a t-shirt!"

Fay couldn't blame her PE teacher for being angry. Her kit had been in the wash since before the half-term holiday. Fay looked helplessly at Mrs Simpson.

"I'm sorry, Miss." Fay could say nothing else. How could she explain?

Mr Parker had spoken to Fay only yesterday about the lack of equipment in her pencil case. He had caught her talking to Chris in class. When Mr Parker told her to tell the class what she was saying, she had to tell everyone that she had been asking to borrow a pen. Mr Parker had already let her borrow school stationery at the start of every week since term began. He was always quick to collect it again at home time on a Friday though. Mr Parker had also told her off for not reading since before half-term; he had taken in the class reading records and noticed that there had been no entries in her book for the past three weeks.

How could she even begin to make him understand?

Now here she was facing a very cross PE teacher, feeling that all the weight of a million problems was resting heavily on her shoulders. Fay didn't want to cry; she wasn't a baby. She didn't want the teachers to be cross with her but she didn't know how to talk about it all.

What should she do?

When Mrs Simpson stopped telling her off, Fay went to watch the rest of the girls practise for Sports Day out on the field. She was not allowed to join in because she wasn't properly dressed for it. After the lesson, she was allowed to leave with the rest of her class to go to lunch, despite Mrs Simpson threatening to keep her back as a 'consequence for her disorganisation'.

Fay found that she couldn't eat. Her stomach churned and tightened and her head was so full of worries that she couldn't focus on what anyone was saying to her. The smell of food made her feel sick and she just knew it would taste like cardboard. She hadn't touched her food at all when a teacher caught her scraping it into the bin. Once again, Fay found herself in front of Mr Parker, probably in trouble. Her stomach felt full of knots as she stood waiting for her telling-off to start.

Mr Parker was silent for so long as he sat alone on the staff dinner table, looking at her carefully, that Fay eventually looked up.

Mr Parker had noticed her uncombed hair and the wrongly buttoned shirt with last week's orange juice stain down the front and he asked her to sit down. He asked if there was anything she wanted to talk about.

At first she didn't know how to begin, but Mr Parker looked so kind and he spoke so softly without anyone else hearing his words that she felt at last that she could tell him that Dad was in hospital. Once she had started, she was able to tell him that she was always having to stay at their neighbour's house and that she was more worried than she had ever been before. She was frightened that her dad might die because he was so ill. She wanted to cry when she saw Nan looking so worried. It had been such a long time since she'd smiled.

The words tumbled from Fay like water flowing off the edge of a waterfall. Mr Parker listened intently. Fay felt good to share her worries and to know that someone else finally understood what she was going through.

So unprepared

What do you think?

1. Why do you think Fay and her nan didn't explain to the school what was happening at home earlier?

2. Would you tell your school if you were in Fay's situation? Explain your answer.

3. What do you think could have been done to make school easier for Fay at this difficult time?

4. What advice would you give to Fay about speaking up?

5. Do you find it easy to talk about your problems? Explain your answer.

6. How do you think your school life would change if someone you loved at home was really ill?

7. Explain whether or not you would still want to go to school as usual if you were in Fay's situation.

8. If you were in a class with someone like Fay with her untidy hair and stained shirt, how would you behave towards them?

9. How do you think Fay's teachers would feel about telling her off if they knew about her worries?

10. List all the reasons you can think of that might explain why someone would come into school as unprepared as Fay.

I can't explain

It was circle time at school and the class had to sit cross-legged in a big circle on the floor and talk about something they'd done over the holiday. Miles hated it. It was bad enough being back in school after summer at the best of times, but today he just didn't feel he could do it.

His classmates loved to talk and had no difficulties chattering on about their summer holidays. Their summers had been filled with fun and trips to the beach or holidays in hotels. Some of them had come back with suntans and had brought their holiday souvenirs and photographs to show off to the rest of the class.

Mum hadn't had time to talk to the teacher this morning but said that she would phone later to explain things. Had she called already? That might mean that Miss Gates would skip over his turn and he wouldn't have to talk. Miles kept his fingers crossed.

Miss Gates continued around the circle. How could he say what was on his mind? His cheeks felt hot and his head started to ache as much as his tummy. As his turn crept closer, Miles started to feel like he wanted to cry.

Miles' mind raced with memories of Nan. She had promised that she would look after him when Mum and Dad had to work in the holidays. He loved it when he went over to her house and they baked cakes together. She always let him lick all the cake mixture off the spoon and out of the bowl. Mum would never let him do that. It was his and Nan's secret.

He had gone to see her with Dad at the start of the holidays. They had rung the bell about ten times but she hadn't answered the door. Dad had to use his key to get in. The curtains were still closed in her house and her tea plates and cup and saucer were still on the side waiting to be washed up. It wasn't like Nan to leave dirty dishes about. Dad had suddenly rushed into Nan's lounge and shouted her name over and over. The telly was on and Nan was sitting in her chair asleep in her nightie, or so it had seemed. She did not wake up when Dad touched her. Dad made a funny noise like he had when he had stubbed his toe on the bathroom door the day before. He quickly took out his mobile and called Mum. His fingers were shaking. His voice sounded sad when he spoke and Miles could hear his Mum cry out on the other end of the phone.

Dad hadn't let Miles go near Nan after that and Auntie Mary from next door arrived to take him to her house. It had been fun. They had gone for a walk with Auntie Mary's dog, Pudgey, and had drawn pictures when they got back to her house. Auntie Mary had even given him his supper before Mum and Dad came to collect him.

Miles remembered that Mum looked different. She wasn't wearing makeup and her eyes were very red. His parents had said that they had something they needed to tell him.

He had cried himself to sleep that night. He still couldn't understand why they were saying that Nan had 'gone' when he'd seen her sitting in her chair. He had lots of hugs from Mum and Dad and they had all cried, but Miles had still wanted to see his nan and reassure himself that she was just asleep in her chair.

It had taken him all of the summer holiday to accept that she really was 'gone'; gone from her house, from her street, from his life. Not seeing her anymore made him very sad. It made his mum sad too because Nan was her mum.

Miles started thinking about how he would feel if his mum was ever 'gone' and it made him cry again.

"What's the matter, Miles? Didn't you like your summer holiday?" Miss Gates' voice broke into his thoughts, her face smiling softly.

"My nan's dead!" Miles blurted out tearfully. The rest of the class gasped and fell silent. Miles' best friend James was sitting next to him and he put his hand on his shoulder to comfort him. Miss Gates put her hand to her mouth.

Miss Gates was kind. She asked her helper to finish circle time and took Miles to the staff room. She made him a drink of squash and gave him one of the teachers' biscuits out of a big tin by the kettle. She gave him a tissue and he gave his nose a big blow. It had been the first time that he had told anyone that his nan was dead.

What do you think?

1. Why do you think people sometimes say 'gone' instead of 'dead'?

2. Do you think that Miles should have been allowed to spend time with his nan when he and his dad found her? Explain your answer.

3. Why do you think that Dad asked Auntie Mary to take Miles to her house for the day? Explain whether you think Dad was right or wrong to do this.

4. Try to explain how it might feel to lose someone you love.

5. Do you know what a funeral is? Try to describe what you think happens at a funeral.

6. If you were friends with Miles, what would you do or say to try to help him feel better?

7. What do you think Miles' school could do to help him cope with the school day?

8. Describe a time when you or a friend have felt upset in school. What happened?

Always there

Mum, you'd always meet me from school with a big smile on your face and a treat in your pocket. It was usually a chocolate bar until that really hot day when you ended up with a pocket full of gooey melted chocolate. You brought me fruit on hot days after that. We'd chat all the way home about how school had gone, about telly, about anything and everything. Then when we got home there'd be a drink ready in the fridge for me and you'd make tea while I did my homework or watched TV.

I remember that when I was very little, we'd snuggle up on the sofa while you read stories to me or we'd colour in my colouring book together. I knew every part of your face; your smile, your eyes, the smell of your skin as you gave me big hugs. Your laughter rang loud and clear throughout the house whenever we were all together at home with family or friends. It was such a lovely sound. You made our house home.

You'd take me shopping and sometimes we'd go for a glass of lemonade and a big chocolate chip cookie in our favourite café in town as a special treat. We'd laugh and talk the whole time and sometimes you'd leave me a piece of your chocolate éclair. My mum, my friend.

I don't remember exactly when it all started to change. Dad had to meet me from school a few times. When I asked him where you were he'd just say you had an appointment and would see me later. The changes were not obvious at first. They happened over time. You seemed sad but I didn't know what was wrong. Your smiles didn't reach your eyes anymore. You didn't talk to me about it and I didn't ask.

Then Dad became sad too and when I asked him why, he cried and squeezed me tight against him for the longest cuddle he had ever given me. I could feel his tears soaking into my shoulder and his chest shake with sobs. I cried too but I didn't know why. My tummy felt full of tight knots and I felt

Always there

alone even though Dad was right there. My head was full of worries that I didn't understand.

Not long afterwards, you went into hospital. Dad and I came to see you. There were machines and wires all around you and I wanted to push them all away so I could get to you and hug you like before. But it was different now. The hospital room seemed full of people in uniforms who asked me not to touch anything. All Dad and I could do was sit there by your bedside watching the rise and fall of your chest, willing you to wake up and chat to us like you always used to. I longed for the sound of your voice to take the place of the beeping machines and the doctors who talked about you as if you weren't there.

Dad and I took flowers to the cemetery for you today. It would have been your birthday. I always used to give you perfume. I would watch your face as you unwrapped it and sprayed it onto your wrist before shoving it under my nose for a good sniff. We always laughed when you did that.

It helps me and Dad to talk about you. We couldn't talk about you for a long time because we used to cry too much. My chest and my tummy still hurt when I remember that we won't see you again, though it's not quite as painful as it was at first. I talk to you all the time, Mum; in my head or out loud in my bedroom. I know you are there with me somewhere. You're always in my thoughts.

I know I am only young, but I understand more than people think I do. I feel older now. I find it hard to play silly games with my friends. Sometimes I feel angry but I don't really know why. I suppose it's because I still miss you. I always will, though talking helps. It helps me to believe that you are still with me, if only in my heart and in my memories. I love you, Mum.

What do you think?

1. Have you ever been to hospital as a patient or a visitor? Describe how you felt when you were there.

2. The child in the story has suffered the death of their much-loved mum and describes feeling 'older' and no longer wanting to play 'silly games' with friends since she died. What do you think Mum would have wanted?

3. When we lose someone we love, it can be very hard to accept what has happened and we may not understand exactly how we feel at first. What do you think you could say or do to help a friend if they had just lost a relative?

4. Why do you think that the child and Dad find it helpful to talk about Mum?

5. Some people find it difficult to talk about the death of a loved one. What advice would you give to someone who finds it hard to explain how they feel?

6. In the story, the child says 'I understand more than people think I do'. Do you ever feel that people do not think you are able to understand grown-up matters because you are young?

7. Why do you think adults don't always tell children everything?

8. Describe or draw a picture of what you think happens to loved ones when they die.

Glad it's not us

"I don't remember!" Mason told the police officer. She was writing down his words; she called it 'taking a statement'. His head ached and his neck still felt sore and stiff. He kept looking over at Mum for help. Mum just smiled, her face covered in bruises.

"I understand, Mason. Please don't worry about the accident. I need you to try to remember what happened before the car crashed," the police officer said. She was being very kind to him and spoke to him in a quiet voice. Mason started to relax.

"Uncle Phil came to take us to the seaside. I was looking forward to it. I love Uncle Phil, he's always lots of fun. He throws me in the air and he remembers to catch me, too!"

Mason paused as he suddenly remembered what Mum had told him this morning. The nurse had just taken his breakfast tray away when Mum arrived at the children's ward in her dressing gown and slippers. She had to sleep on the women's ward. Mum had told him that Uncle Phil had been very badly injured in the crash. She said that Dad had stayed with him all night but this morning, Uncle Phil had gone. Mason had to ask her where he'd gone. Mum had found it hard to say the word 'died' and as soon as she said it, Mason wished she hadn't. He had only just finished crying when the police officer turned up. He didn't really feel like talking.

"Mason? Are you alright?" Mum had come to sit on his bed. She took his hand, the one that wasn't attached to a tube.

"Yes, but Uncle Phil isn't, is he? I won't see Uncle Phil again, will I?" Mason looked searchingly at his mum, willing her to say she'd been joking or that the hospital had made a mistake and that really Uncle Phil was fit and healthy and waiting for them at home. But she didn't.

"Perhaps you could come back tomorrow? I don't think this is the right time,"

Mum said to the police officer. Mason was glad. He felt exhausted and sick. His head and neck hurt and he just wanted to be with his mum.

The police officer left.

"Mum?" Mason asked from the folds of Mum's dressing gown as she cuddled him on his bed.

"Yes, love?"

"Uncle Phil was driving the car with his knees, wasn't he? He always likes to do that and he laughs and shouts 'Look! No hands!' and then he grabs the wheel again. That's what he was doing, isn't it?" Mason asked his mum.

Mum sat up, unsure of what to say to her son. Phil had always been a joker and he'd do anything for a laugh. He'd settled down a lot lately though and she had agreed to let him drive them to the beach; herself, Mason and her husband Dave. She had thought that it would be alright. She was wrong.

She was in the back of the car with Mason, and Dave was in the passenger seat. She had noticed how fast Phil was driving. They were all being thrown to one side and then the other as he swerved around the bends in the roads. He had been overtaking other cars when he couldn't possibly have known that nothing was coming the other way. He was messing about, telling jokes and turning around to wink at Mason in the back seat. She had made the mistake of asking him to drive slower and look where he was going as he turned down the back road towards the fishing village. Phil had just thought it funny that she had 'told him off' and had teased her that she was getting too old to have fun. He had taken his hands off the steering wheel for just a few seconds and looked around at Mason to see his reaction. He hadn't seen the tractor coming out of the gateway in front of them.

Mum remembered screaming, she remembered

Phil looking towards the tractor and shouting, she remembered him practically standing on the brake, she remembered looking at the back of his head as the car lurched forward. Phil had swerved too sharply and hit a tree. Then there was silence. They had all survived the accident but Phil was so badly injured they knew he might not make it. He hadn't. He had died at four o'clock that morning with his brother at his bedside.

"Mum? Don't cry. I don't have to tell the police lady that Uncle Phil wasn't being a good driver!"

"It's okay, Mason. Don't worry. We have to tell the police lady what we remember. We must be honest."

Mason was glad his mum was with him. He felt so ill and shaky. His tummy was feeling upset and sore and he didn't understand how he felt about Uncle Phil dying. He felt guilty because he was relieved that it was not his mum or dad who had died. He felt guilty that if Uncle Phil had not turned to look at him he would have seen the tractor in time to stop. He was sad that he would never see Uncle Phil again. He loved Uncle Phil and had been worried about telling on him to the police officer. Mason's head was aching with the weight of his jumbled thoughts.

Burying his head in his mum's dressing gown, Mason let out another shudder as his tears fell. Mum had said it was okay to tell the truth about Uncle Phil, and Mason knew it was the right thing to do.

What do you think?

1. Why do you think Mason was so worried about telling the police officer about Uncle Phil's driving?

2. Mum tells Mason that they must tell the truth to the police. Why do you think this is important?

3. Think about how Uncle Phil behaved when he was driving. Have you or someone you know ever behaved in a silly way that made you or them forget any possible dangers?

4. Why do you think Uncle Phil behaved how he did when he was driving?

5. Would you ever get into a car with someone you knew to be a dangerous driver? Explain your answer.

6. Uncle Phil was Mason's dad's brother. Do you think Dad should have said anything to him about the way he was driving? Explain whether or not you think this would have made a difference.

7. Mason feels guilty about feeling relieved that his mum and dad survived the accident when Uncle Phil didn't. What do you think is meant by the word 'guilty'?

8. Do you think Mason should feel guilty? Explain your answer.

9. Describe something that has made you feel guilty or confused and try to explain why it made you feel like this.

10. How do you think that Mason's life will change as a result of the car accident and the loss of his uncle?

He shouldn't do that

Jamie loved his bike. He loved the feeling of the wind against his face as he shot down the hill on it. It was fab! He promised himself all day in school that as soon as he got in he'd ask his mum to let him go on his bike before dinner.

Mum was already in the kitchen making dinner when he walked in and dumped his bag in the hall. He asked her if he could go out straight away.

"You've only got about forty minutes before tea's ready. I want you back in half an hour so you'll have time to wash your hands. Oh, and no wandering off, remember what I told you – stay on the estate so I can find you if I need you," Mum told him. She kissed him on the head and ruffled his hair with her hand.

"Bye, Mum!" Jamie shouted as he went out the back door to collect his bike from the shed.

Closing the gate behind him, he paused for a moment to get his helmet on. It looked like it might rain but he didn't care about that. He got on his bike and pedalled furiously until he got to the top of the hill and then felt the full force of the wind against him as he freewheeled all the way down it. When he reached the bottom, he turned right to go round the block and back to the top of the hill, pedalling faster and faster until he reached the top. As he set off again, he let himself speed up even more on the downward slope. He managed three goes before his mum called him in for tea. He'd lost track of the time.

The following evening, he went out on his bike again, but there were some older boys out too. Jamie felt a little scared of them because he didn't know them. He really wanted to ride his bike somewhere though, so he turned left at the bottom of the hill instead of right and ended up on the estate next to his. The hill wasn't as steep but it would do, he supposed. He was enjoying himself until he got a puncture just off a driveway belonging to one of the smaller houses on the estate. His bike suddenly swerved and the front wheel turned sharply, tugging the handle bars out of his hands. The bike skidded along the gravelled surface of the driveway and Jamie was thrown off. He came to rest against a wheelie bin. He was dazed and confused at first and then slowly realised that not only was he going to have to wheel his bike all the way home, but that his mum would be ready to explode if she knew he wasn't on his own estate.

Just then a man appeared next to him on the driveway.

"Are you alright, son? Give me your hand and I'll help you up."

The man was as old as Grandad and sounded very concerned. Jamie gave him his grazed hand and was pulled to his feet.

"Thank you." Jamie wobbled a little and his head felt heavy, but he was surprisingly unhurt after such a horrible accident.

"Let me help you. I can fix your bike and I think I've got some plasters in the house," the man said. He had already picked up the bike and was carrying it towards the house as he spoke.

In the kitchen, the man ran water into a bowl for Jamie to wash his grazed hands and then fixed the puncture in his front tyre. Jamie was very grateful and thanked the man at least four times.

It was getting late by the time the puncture was fixed and Jamie started to worry about his mum. He was already expected home at least fifteen minutes ago and he knew she would be getting worried.

"I'd better go now," Jamie said, rising to his feet. The man rose too.

"Who knows where you are?" the man asked. Jamie thought this was a strange question and didn't answer it.

"I'm late and I've got school tomorrow," Jamie told the man as he made his way towards the door.

"You could stay here if you like. Who wants to go to school anyway? We could have fun together instead. Do you have a girlfriend? I bet you do, you're

He shouldn't do that

a good-looking lad. Where do you live?" The man had followed Jamie to the door but instead of opening it for him, he leant against it, blocking Jamie from getting out.

"I'd better go, but thank you again." Jamie grabbed the door handle but couldn't open it against the weight of the man's body leaning against the door.

"You don't have to leave. I'll give your mum a call for you and explain how hurt you are and then I'll run you home in my car. It'll be no trouble." The man spoke in soft, soothing tones and he rested his hand on Jamie's waist as he reached inside his cardigan pocket for his mobile.

Jamie seized his chance. While the man's attention was focused on his mobile phone, Jamie ran to the back door and threw it open. He ran as fast as he could all the way home, leaving his bike behind. At that moment, all he wanted was to get away.

When he got home, Mum was too worried about where he'd been to be cross and he told her everything that had happened. He was a little scared when she told him that she was going to call the police, but she reassured him that she only needed some advice on how to get the bike back.

Later that evening, Mum came into Jamie's bedroom with a glass of milk and a biscuit. Now, sitting in the safety of his own room with the soft orange glow from his bedside lamp and his mum on the edge of his bed, Jamie realised how lucky he had been.

The police had told Mum that the man who had offered him help had been in trouble with them before. Mum didn't go into detail but she sounded angry and upset when she was telling him.

Jamie had been confused at first. The man had been so helpful and kind, how could he be a bad person? Then he remembered the way he had touched him on the waist, the things he had said and how his voice had changed because he had wanted him to stay. Jamie wondered what would have happened to him if he hadn't been able to leave. He shuddered and promised himself that he would never stray from where his mum knew he was again and would never go into a stranger's house. Jamie realised that anything could have happened today.

What do you think?

1. Why do you think it is important to always go home at the time you're expected?

2. Jamie left his estate even though his mum had asked him to stay close to home. List all of the things that could have happened to him.

3. Have you or someone you know ever wandered away from where grown-ups would know where to find you? Describe what happened.

4. If you were Jamie, would you have been happy to accept help from the man in the story? Explain your answer.

5. What do you know about stranger danger?

6. Have you or your friends ever been afraid of a grown-up? Why?

7. If a grown-up ever did something to you or spoke to you in a way that made you feel uncomfortable or confused, what would you do about it?

8. Why do you think Jamie felt scared when Mum told him she was going to call the police?

9. Why do you think Mum sounded angry and upset as she was explaining that the man had been in trouble with the police before?

10. What lessons do you think Jamie has learned from his encounter with the man?

Dreading it

Lee watched the others playing as he sat alone. They were running around being soldiers, hiding from each other, pretending to fall down dead and then clambering to their feet. They were smiling, laughing, having fun.

Break was nearly over. Lee had been sat alone the whole time. He hadn't bothered to open his lunchbox; there was no point. It was always the same biscuit. It was usually soft and tasted of cardboard. The packet in the kitchen cupboard had been open for ages. He just didn't fancy it today.

Charlie and Max were rolling on the floor in a play-fight and the other boys were cheering them on. Miss Barker was on her way over to them to break it up. Lee didn't feel like he was part of it. He had forgotten how to smile or laugh and their games seemed like too much effort, too silly. Miss Barker was telling the boys off and Charlie was crying, his face covered in mud and his lip cut. Lee hated the sight of blood now. He stayed where he was, his back resting against the tree, dampness from the grass seeping into his trousers. He didn't have the energy to move. Miss Barker was about to take Charlie and Max up to see the headteacher and noticed Lee as she glanced over. She smiled. Lee smiled back weakly. She turned and, still shouting, marched the boys towards the school building. The rest of the gang wandered off, leaving Lee alone with only his tangled thoughts for company; thoughts that he tried to block out but always crept back.

At the end of the day, Miss Barker helped him into his coat. She jokingly told him his coat was a bit big and laughed that she couldn't see his whole hand as half of it was still up his sleeve. When Nan had bought his coat for him, it had been a perfect fit. She had come to stay before Christmas when Dad was working away. When Nan had stayed, the house smelled of cooking and furniture polish and he hadn't had to step over dirty clothes to get from room to room. Lee hadn't liked having to have a bath every night but Nan had teased him about having smelly feet so he had put up with the bedtime routine. It had been nice having

Nan to stay. Dad wasn't supposed to find out that she'd been; it was to be their secret.

When Nan had gone, Dad had come home in a bad mood and said that the house was too tidy and Mum looked too nice. He had asked her who she had been trying to impress while he was away. The row lasted for days and eventually Mum had screamed at him that Nan had been staying, just to stop him going on about it. Lee had wondered before if Nan only visited when Dad was away because he would have found it too difficult to be on his best behaviour in front of her. Now he realised it was because Dad didn't like Nan and the way she 'stuck her nose in'. That was what Lee thought he'd heard during the argument anyway. Nan lived so far away, Lee knew he wouldn't see her again for months. He felt like crying again and took a deep breath to try to stop himself from thinking about it.

Lee waited in the classroom for his mum to collect him. He could see out of the window as he waited with the other children for his name to be called. Little groups of mums and dads with baby brothers and sisters in pushchairs were standing around the playground, talking and laughing. Lee didn't feel like he belonged to the world; it seemed too happy. Gradually the classroom emptied and eventually just one woman stood alone, swaying slightly, steadying herself on the fencepost to keep her balance. Lee walked slowly outside, not knowing what to expect. It would depend on whether or not he could smell beer. It was a smell he dreaded.

As he got closer, Mum shouted her goodbyes to his teacher, her words slurred. He could see the fresh bruise on her cheek and the cut on her top lip. Dad must be home. The door behind him slammed, shutting him out of school and normality. His stomach was growling restlessly with hunger and anxiety, his heart was thumping and his body was shivering with cold. He was dreading going home.

Dreading it

What do you think?

1. Why do you think Lee only had a biscuit in his lunchbox?

2. Why do you think Lee doesn't join in with the other children anymore?

3. If Lee was in your class, do you think you would know that he was feeling sad?

4. Do you think any of Lee's teachers should have realised that something is wrong with him? Explain your answer.

5. How do you feel when you are worried about something?

6. Why do you think Lee is dreading going home?

7. List all the reasons you can think of that could explain why someone like Lee's dad would be nasty to his mum. Do you think this behaviour is ever justified?

8. What do you think Mum could do to make things better for herself and Lee?

9. Do you think Lee could do anything about the situation he is in?

10. Draw a picture of Lee as he is leaving school. Add a thought bubble to show what he is thinking.

INDEX

abuse, child   92
abuse, domestic   96
aggression   12, 23, 51, 61, 65, 76, 96
anger   23, 42, 51, 61, 65, 76, 96
anxiety   12, 20, 30, 47, 51, 69, 73, 76, 79, 82, 88, 96

body image   9, 15, 20, 42, 45
bullying   6, 9, 12, 15, 23, 51, 61, 65

death   82, 85, 88
divorce   73

eczema   15

fighting   23, 51, 61, 65
friendship   2, 6, 12, 15, 20, 30, 47, 51, 61, 69

gender identity   42, 45
graffiti   54
grief   82, 85
guilt   6, 30, 88

head lice   9
home circumstances   9, 27, 47, 73, 79, 96

illness   2, 27, 79, 85
injury   30, 33, 36, 39, 51, 65, 76, 88, 92, 96

jealousy   2

lying   2, 20, 23, 27, 30, 58

neglect   79, 96

obesity   20

paedophilia   92
parents, relationships with   33, 39, 42, 47, 58, 65, 73, 76, 85, 88, 96
personal hygiene   9, 79
police   30, 88, 92
pyromania   39

safety, fire   36, 39
safety, road   33, 88
school, absence from   2, 27, 30
school, new   2, 47, 69
school, truancy from   27, 30
self-defence   12, 23, 51, 92
self-harm   76
sexuality   47
sharing   2, 6
social skills   2, 6, 9, 12, 15, 20, 47, 51, 61, 65, 96
stealing   39, 58
stranger danger   92

teasing   9, 15, 20, 23

vandalism   54
video games   65
violence   51, 65, 96